Growing a Godly Marriage
and Raising Godly Children

by David E. Pratte

Available in print at
www.gospelway.com/sales

Growing a Godly Marriage and Raising Godly Children

ISBN-13: 978-1492359425
ISBN-10: 1492359424

Note carefully: No teaching in any of our materials is intended or should ever be construed to justify or to in any way incite or encourage personal vengeance or physical violence against any person.

"He who glories, let him glory in the Lord" – 1 Corinthians 1:31

Cover photo: Public domain

Other Acknowledgements

Unless otherwise indicated, Scripture quotations are generally from the New King James Version (NKJV), copyright 1982, 1988 by Thomas Nelson, Inc. used by permission. All rights reserved.

Scripture quotations marked (NASB) are from *Holy Bible, New American Standard* La Habra, CA: The Lockman Foundation, 1995.

Scripture quotations marked (ESV) are from *The Holy Bible, English Standard Version*, copyright ©2001 by Crossway Bibles, a publishing ministry of Good News Publishers. Used by permission. All rights reserved.

Scripture quotations marked (MLV) are from Modern Literal Version of The New Testament, Copyright 1999 by G. Allen Walker.

Scripture quotations marked (NRSV) are from the New Revised Standard Version of the Bible, copyright 1989 by the Division of Christian Education, National Council of the Churches of Christ in the United States of America.

Scripture quotations marked (NIV) are from the New International Version of the Holy Bible, copyright 1978 by Zondervan Bible publishers, Grand Rapids, Michigan.

Scripture quotations marked (HCSB) are from the Holman Christian Standard Bible, copyright 2008 by Holman Bible publishers, Nashville, Tennessee.

Other Books by the Author

Topical Bible Studies

Why Believe in God, Jesus, and the Bible? (evidences)
True Words of God: Bible Inspiration and Preservation
"It Is Written": The Authority of the Bible
Salvation through Jesus Christ: Basics of Forgiveness
Grace, Faith, and Obedience: The Gospel or Calvinism?
Growing a Godly Marriage & Raising Godly Children
The God of the Bible (study of the Father, Son, and Holy Spirit)
Kingdom of Christ: Future Millennium or Present Spiritual Reign?
Do Not Sin Against the Child: Abortion, Unborn Life, & the Bible

Commentaries on Bible Books

Genesis	*Proverbs*	*Ephesians*
Joshua and Ruth	*Ecclesiastes*	*Philippians &*
Judges	*Gospel of Matthew*	*Colossians*
1 Samuel	*Gospel of Mark*	*1 & 2 Thessalonians*
2 Samuel	*Gospel of John*	*Hebrews*
1 Kings	*Acts*	*James and Jude*
2 Kings	*Romans*	*1 and 2 Peter*
Ezra, Nehemiah, Esther	*Galatians*	*1,2,3 John*
Job		

Bible Question Class Books

Genesis	*Ecclesiastes*	*2 Corinthians and*
Joshua and Ruth	*Isaiah*	*Galatians*
Judges	*Daniel*	*Ephesians and*
1 Samuel	*Hosea, Joel, Amos,*	*Philippians*
2 Samuel	*Obadiah*	*Colossians, 1&2*
1 Kings	*Gospel of Matthew*	*Thessalonians*
2 Kings	*Gospel of Mark*	*1 & 2 Timothy,*
Ezra, Nehemiah,	*Gospel of Luke*	*Titus, Philemon*
Esther	*Gospel of John*	*Hebrews*
Job	*Acts*	*James – Jude*
Proverbs	*Romans*	*Revelation*
	1 Corinthians	

Workbooks with Study Notes

Jesus Is Lord: Workbook on the Fundamentals of the Gospel of Christ
Following Jesus: Workbook on Discipleship
God's Eternal Purpose in Christ: Workbook on the Theme of the Bible
Family Reading Booklist

Visit our website at <u>www.gospelway.com/sales</u> to see a current list of books in print.

Growing a Godly Marriage

Other Resources from the Author

Table of Contents

(Due to printer reformatting, the above numbers may be off a page or two.)

Notes to the Reader

Unless otherwise indicated, Bible quotations are from the New King James Version. Often – especially when I do not use quotations marks – I am not quoting any translation but simply paraphrasing the passage in my own words.

You may find that major topics of this material will repeat topics or concepts covered elsewhere (such as love and authority). This serves to emphasize these points and allows each major topic of study to be complete of itself (so major sections can be studied independently).

To join our mailing list to be informed of new books or special sales, contact the author at
www.gospelway.com/comments

Marriage Preparation and Improvement

Introduction

There is significant evidence that many marriages today are troubled.

Many forces in society are undermining the Biblical concept of the home.

* **Divorce** – Each year the number of divorces is about half the number of marriages.

* **Conflict and violence** – Many families quarrel continually or even become violent. Nearly 1/3 of all murders are committed between family members.

* **Fornication and sexual unfaithfulness** – Premarital sex and even extra-marital sex are commonly accepted.

* **Rebellious and delinquent children** – Many young people rebel against the moral or religious standards taught them by their parents.

* **Confusion about authority and roles in the home** – We are told that it is old-fashioned for parents to insist that their children obey them or to use physical punishment to motivate their children. Society often opposes belief in separate roles for husbands and wives (husband as breadwinner and family leader, and wife as homemaker).

It follows that a study of marriage should be valuable to everyone.

* **Couples who are engaged or seriously considering marriage** should appreciate guidance about how to have a good

marriage and how to determine whether or not they are suited for one another.

    * **Individuals, who hope to marry someday** and may be looking for somebody, need to consider how to prepare for marriage and how to choose a marriage partner.

    * **People who are already married** need to consider how to improve their marriage.

    * **Unmarried people – even if they never plan to marry –** can still profit from such a study, because they are surrounded by married people who may need encouragement. As Christians, we should all try to help other people understand God's will for their homes.

The purpose of this study is to discuss a number of basic principles to help people prepare for marriage or improve marriage.

    I do not profess to know all about marriage, but I believe God understands marriage and has revealed the best plan for marriage. I surely do not claim to have been a perfect husband or father. On the contrary, I know many areas where I have failed or could have improved, and my family can probably name other areas that I am not aware of. So, the goal is to study what the Bible says about marriage, and perhaps along the way I can help you avoid some of my mistakes.

    Whether we seek to prepare for marriage or to improve our marriage, here are important areas we need to consider:

The Role of Religion

Religion is important in the home in all of the following areas:

The Authority or Source of Guidance
Your Home Follows

Many people are confused about the proper way to conduct their home life. What authority should your home follow?

People often follow human "authorities" to the harm of the home.

Worldly marriage "experts" – many consult psychiatrists, feminists, sex educators, civil government, etc. (1 Corinthians 1:19-21; 2:4,5; Proverbs 14:12)

Practices of society – we may follow the advice or example of friends, neighbors, etc. (Romans 12:1,2; 2 Corinthians 10:12; Matthew 7:13,14)

Practices of our parents – people tend to act in their families the way people around them acted as they grew up. (Matthew 10:34-37; Acts 5:29)

Personal desires or desires of family members (Matthew 16:24,25; 10:34-37)

We need not ignore all advice these sources give; they are not always mistaken. But they are often wrong, and many problems in our homes come from following such sources of information.

We need a better standard – a source of higher wisdom. Suppose we had an infallible source of guidance. Shouldn't we follow such a standard, instead of these fallible human standards? If these human guides disagree with our infallible source, shouldn't we reject the human standards and follow the infallible one?

The ultimate source of guidance in your home should be the Bible.

Genesis 2:18-24 – God created marriage and the home from the beginning. Since He created marriage, He knows the best way to conduct it.

2 Timothy 3:16,17 – Scriptures are profitable to teach and instruct us and provide us completely to all good works. Doesn't that include the good work of having a good marriage?

Isaiah 55:8,9 – But God's wisdom is superior to that of man, like the heavens are higher than the earth. This is true in every area, including marriage.

Joshua 1:8 – We have success when we study God's plan and do not depart from it. Many claim to believe this regarding salvation, the church, worship, etc. But do we likewise follow God's plan for our homes? (Matthew 15:9)

Psalm 127:1 – Except the Lord builds the house, they labor in vain that build it.

We do not need to have so much confusion and uncertainty about family affairs. The Bible is the word of God, and God is never wrong. If you want a good marriage and a good home, you must follow the proper guide.

(1 Thessalonians 2:13; 2 Peter 1:3; Acts 17:11)

The Main Goal for Our Homes

Too many families put too much emphasis on materialistic goals.

Material possessions – Luke 12:15-21; 1 Timothy 6:9,10; 1 John 2:15-17

Pleasure – 2 Timothy 3:1-5; Hebrews 11:24-26

Popularity and social standing – John 12:42,43

Beauty and appearance – Proverbs 31:30; 1 Peter 3:3,4

Recreation and athletics – 1 Timothy 4:8

The most important goal our homes should seek to accomplish is to serve God and to help one another receive eternal life.

Genesis 18:19 – Abraham commanded his house to keep God's ways.

Joshua 24:15 – Joshua committed himself and his family to serve God.

Malachi 2:15 – God seeks homes that result in godly offspring.

There are other important goals for our homes, such as love and companionship and raising our children to be good citizens. But even if a family has all these, it is still a failure if it does not accomplish the most important goal. Too often families become so involved in pursuing other less important goals that they neglect responsibilities to God.

In order to have proper home lives, service to God must be our main focal point. Do not marry someone who does not view serving God as their main goal in life.

(Matthew 6:33; Romans 12:1,2; 1 Corinthians 15:58)

The Importance of Worshiping God and Studying His Word in our Homes

Our families should worship God together.

Genesis 2:18-24 – A man and his wife should be companions for one another. If serving God is our most important goal in life, then worship is one important area that we should share.

Joshua 24:15 – Joshua determined that he and his house would serve the Lord. This is something the whole family together was committed to doing.

John 4:23,24; Hebrews 10:24,25 – God wants His people to worship Him, including attending church assemblies. If we are to help one another serve Him, then we will do this together.

Young couples, from the very beginning of their relationship, should determine to attend every meeting of the local church and take advantage of other opportunities to worship. If someone is not interested in worshiping God with you, what are the chances that you can work with that person to help one another serve God?

If you want a good marriage and a good home, you must worship God regularly together.

To be guided by God's word, a family must study it together.

Hebrews 3:13 – Christians should exhort one another daily to stay faithful. But helping one another serve God is the main goal of our homes. We cannot possibly accomplish the most important purpose for our marriage unless we daily study and discuss God's word.

Genesis 18:19 – Abraham commanded his family to keep God's way.

Deuteronomy 6:6-9 – We should keep God's words in our hearts, teaching them diligently to our children, talking of them continually. (Ephesians 6:4)

Young couples should study and discuss Bible subjects from the beginning of their relationship. This helps you understand one another's beliefs, develops your Bible knowledge, and establishes a spiritual foundation for your relationship. If someone is not comfortable or not interested in studying the Bible with you, what are the chances he/she will work with you to achieve the ultimate goal of serving God and going to heaven?

If you want a good marriage and a good home, you must learn to discuss God's word together.

(1 Thessalonians 5:11; Acts 8:4; 10:24,27,33)

In particular, families need to pray together and pray for one another.

James 5:16 – Praying together is one of the most important things Christians can do to help one another be saved. But remember, helping one another be saved is the main goal of marriage.

James 1:5 – Those who need wisdom should pray for it. This wisdom will come as you study God's word. But don't you need wisdom to have a good marriage? Are there things about your marriage that you wish you had the wisdom to improve? Do you want to know whether or not it would be wise to marry some particular young man/woman? If so, then you must diligently pray that you will have wisdom from God's word. (Hebrews 5:14)

Philippians 4:6 – Be anxious for nothing, but in everything by prayer and supplication, with thanksgiving, let your requests be made known to God. Don't we often have concerns for our marriage and our family? Do we become anxious or worried about what might happen? Don't we have needs we wish to see fulfilled in our homes? Then let us pray to God about these things.

Genesis 24:12 – When Abraham gave his servant a charge to find a wife for Isaac, the servant went to God in prayer for success. Do you want success for yourself or your children in finding a marriage companion? If Abraham's servant prayed about this decision, shouldn't you do the same?

Again, I urge young couples to begin this practice from the very early days of your relationship. If someone is not comfortable praying with you or does not think prayer is important, will he/she make a good marriage companion?

Every Christian who wants a good marriage should pray every day for himself, his spouse, and his children, that all will serve God faithfully. If you want a good marriage and a good home, you must pray to God regularly.

(1 Chronicles 29:19)

The Importance of Common Faith in the Home

Genesis 2:18 – One of the most important purposes of marriage is companionship: sharing common goals and interests. Failure to share a common religious faith is one of the major grounds for conflict in marriage.

A Christian should marry a faithful Christian for all the following reasons:

A faithful Christian will help, not hinder, your worship to God.

John 4:23,24; Hebrews 10:24,25 – We already learned that families should worship God together, especially attending public worship assemblies. When both companions are Christians, they commune together in song, prayer, the Lord's Supper, etc. They will agree about the need to give generously to support the church.

But if you do not marry a Christian, your spouse may not attend with you. Worse yet, he or she may attend a false religious group. He may actively oppose your attendance with the Lord's church. He may resent and oppose giving money to church.

Proverbs 15:8,29 – Even if your companion does not actively oppose your worship, you still lack the unity and support you need. God will not accept his worship as long as he remains outside Christ. (1 Corinthians 10:16,17)

A faithful Christian will pray with you, not hinder your prayers.

We have learned that Christians should pray to God together and pray for one another (James 5:16; 1 Thessalonians 5:17).

1 John 3:22 – But if your companion is not a Christian, God will not hear or answer his prayer (Proverbs 28:9; James 5:16). He may even ridicule you for your prayers. If a young lady marries a young man who is not a Christian, who will lead family prayers before meals and other times when Christians would pray together?

A faithful Christian will help, not hinder, your Bible study.

We have also learned that Christian couples should discuss and study Bible principles together and encourage one another with God's word (Hebrews 3:13; 1 Thessalonians 5:11).

But a companion who is not a Christian may not be willing to study. If you initiate a spiritual discussion, the result may be argument and conflict. In all these aspects of worship, instead of being a source of strength, your companion will become a hindrance and discouragement.

A faithful Christian will help, not hinder, your efforts to teach God's word.

Acts 8:4 – Christians should share the message of the gospel with others (Hebrews 5:12). This too is something we can help one another do in our homes (Acts 10:24,27,33).

Acts 18:26 – Like Aquila and Priscilla, Christian couples work together in this, inviting friends over to discuss religion and study the Bible. They can talk together and share ideas to improve their teaching.

But if your companion is not a Christian, he may oppose your efforts to teach. He may object if you invite others to your home to study, and may resent the time you spend in teaching. He may openly contradict the truth, and will surely hinder your teaching by his example.

Growing a Godly Marriage

A faithful Christian will obey and help you obey Bible teaching about marriage.

We have learned that truly good marriages must be based on Bible principles. Most marital unhappiness comes because people do not follow the Bible principles about marriage.

We will learn more about these principles as we proceed: husbands should love and provide for their wives, wives should submit to their husbands and be homemakers, etc.

If you marry a Christian, you have a right to expect him or her to obey the Bible. But you would have no reason from the very outset to expect a non-Christian to obey God's word. If he or she does not obey God's plan for marriage, how will you motivate him to do right?

A faithful Christian will encourage, not discourage, proper morality.

2 Timothy 3:16,17; Psalm 119:105 – Christian couples have a common standard by which to determine their moral beliefs and practices.

But if you marry one who is not a Christian, he may have (or may develop) habits you object to: drinking liquor, smoking, profanity, dirty jokes, gambling, dirty TV shows, suggestive clothing, even pornography or drug abuse.

What if he/she spends family funds on things you consider to be immoral? What if he/she is dishonest in business dealings or refuses to pay family debts? What if he wants to donate funds to causes that you oppose?

How can you appeal to him, if you knew all along that he was not living by the Bible?

A faithful Christian will help, not hinder, your relations with friends and in-laws.

1 Corinthians 15:33 – Evil companions corrupt our morals. When you marry, you inherit your companion's family and friends. If you marry a faithful Christian, he will want to associate with Christians and good moral people.

But if you marry one who is not a Christian, his closest friends will not be Christians. And what about in-laws? Will your in-laws oppose your religious beliefs? How well will you get along with them, and how well will he get along with your family and friends?

You need to seriously consider these questions before marriage. (Proverbs 13:20; 29:27)

A Christian will work with you, not against you, in raising your children.

Nearly all the concerns we have already discussed become magnified when the children come along. Each spouse wants the children raised in agreement with his or her views.

Ephesians 6:4; Genesis 18:19; Deuteronomy 6:4-9; Proverbs 22:6 – Christians will agree to train the children "in the nurture and admonition of the Lord." They will work together in regular Bible study and bringing the children to all the assemblies of the church (Hebrews 10:25).

But if you do not marry a Christian, your companion may discourage your children from studying the Bible, attending services, or becoming Christians. He or she may even insist that the children go with him to attend a false church or allow them to attend recreational or social activities instead of church meetings.

Proverbs 13:24 – Parents who are Christians have a standard for agreeing what moral principles they will teach their children. They will agree to chastise the children, firmly and consistently in love, to motivate them to obey (Hebrews 12:5-11).

But if your companion is not a Christian, what will you do if he or she allows the children to drink, smoke, dress immodestly, use profanity, attend dances, go to wild parties, run with a bad crowd, or even share a bedroom with a friend of the opposite sex? What will you do if he refuses to punish the children when they need it, or if he opposes your efforts to discipline the children?

Nehemiah 13:23,24 – When Israelites married people of other nations and religions, the heathen parents influenced the children. Likewise, your non-Christian spouse will influence your children.

Raising children is difficult enough, even when the parents work together. How will you feel if one of your children is eternally lost because you chose to marry a non-Christian?

A Christian will help, not hinder, your efforts to achieve your most important goal: serving God and receiving eternal life.

Matthew 6:33 – We already learned that helping one another serve God should be the most important goal of marriage. If you marry a Christian, he or she will share with you this major goal. But if you marry someone who is not a Christian, then he or she will not share with you the most important area of your life.

Revelation 20:14,15 – Anyone not found in the Book of Life will be sent into the lake of fire, the second death. Your spouse should be the dearest loved one on earth to you. If he or she is not a Christian, then you face the great likelihood that your dearest loved one will be lost eternally! Will you be able to live with that fact without compromising the truth to please him or her?

Nehemiah 13:26,27 – The Old Testament forbade marriage to people of other nations, because it would lead God's people into sin. Solomon was an example of one to whom this happened (Deuteronomy 7:3,4). We do not live under the Old Testament, but the danger still exists.

You and your potential spouse need to thoroughly discuss all such concerns *early in your relationship*. If your companion promises he/she will change, give them plenty of time to prove they are willing to change *before making any commitment about marriage*. And give it long enough you are convinced the change will last.

If your marriage is to be happy and successful, you will need to go through life working with another faithful Christian.

(Matthew 16:24-27; Romans 12:1,2; John 6:27,63; Luke 12:15-21; 14:26; Matthew 10:34-37)

The Purpose of Marriage

If we understand the proper purposes for marriage, we are far more likely to accomplish those goals and to choose a mate with whom we can accomplish them. If we do not understand those goals, we are almost sure to fail to achieve what marriage is about.

The Main Goal of Marriage Is to Help One Another Serve God.

We have already discussed this under "Religion." However, there are also other legitimate reasons for marrying.

Marriage Should Provide Companionship and Love.

Genesis 2:18,21,22 – Woman was created because it was not good for man to be alone. The animals were not suitable companions for man, so God created woman to be his companion and helper. (Proverbs 18:22; 19:14)

Malachi 2:14 – The wife is a **companion** with whom the man has entered into the marriage covenant. (Proverbs 2:17)

Ephesians 5:25-29; Titus 2:4 – Husband and wife are both instructed to **love** one another.

When man and wife are proper companions, loving one another as the Bible teaches, they fulfill one of the strongest desires and greatest needs people have. Do not marry until you are ready to love and care for your spouse at least as much as you care for yourself. However, this requires understanding what love really is. We will discuss this later in depth.

Marriage Should Bear and Raise Children.

Genesis 1:27,28; 2:24 – God told the first man and woman to reproduce and replenish the earth. This should be done in the marriage relationship.

Psalms 127:3-5; 128:1-6 – Children should be appreciated as gifts from God.

Malachi 2:15 – God makes man and woman one, because He seeks godly offspring.

Ephesians 6:4 – Parents have a duty, in the family, to raise and train the children they bring into the world (Genesis 3:16).

No other institution or arrangement can produce the same benefits for children as can the family. This is one reason why it is immoral to bear children out of wedlock or to refuse to care for them after we have given them birth. If children can be raised acceptably by child-care arrangements or government facilities, why did God insist that they be raised in a family?

One of life's greatest fulfillments is the sense of accomplishment that comes from knowing you have brought up children who honor God and are a blessing to people around them. Young couples should not marry unless both parties are willing to make the sacrifices and put forth the effort to do the very best they can to achieve this goal.

Marriage Should Provide Sexual Affection.

Hebrews 13:4 – The sexual union is holy and pure only within marriage.

Proverbs 5:15-20 – Man should find fulfillment for his desires only in his lawful wife.

1 Corinthians 7:2-5,8,9 – Husband and wife should express sexual affection, not tempting the spouse by "defrauding" them. Satisfying this desire is one legitimate reason for getting married.

Note that the sexual union is **not** just for procreation. It is a basic urge created by God. It is pure and holy, but it can properly be fulfilled only within the God-ordained institution of marriage. So, it becomes a natural expression of the love and companionship of marriage.

Most people marry for a combination of the above reasons. When we understand the proper reasons for marriage, we also understand why it is a mistake to marry for other reasons, such as:

* To attain wealth, influence, popularity, or social status
* To escape serious problems in one's previous home life
* Because all one's friends are getting married
* Just to feel that somebody wants us – some people have felt unloved and rejected or inferior all their lives, so they just want to feel like somebody wants them.
* Because we are "on the rebound" from a broken relationship

* Because we want someone to provide for us or to keep house for us, etc.

* Because our family or friends think we make a good couple

When people enter marriage for these improper reasons, they usually find their marriage dissatisfies them, their companions, and especially God.

Marriage is without doubt one of the most important decisions of life. Before you marry, be sure you and your prospective spouse understand the proper purposes of marriage.

Growing a Godly Marriage

The Permanence of Marriage

Divorce is a terrible tragedy leaving husbands, wives, and especially children emotionally scarred for life. Often there are also severe financial consequences, especially for the wife and children. Above all, divorce always involves someone in disobedience to God.

Bible Teaching

Genesis 2:24 – From the beginning, God intended marriage to consist of one man and one woman who **cleave** (are "joined" – NKJV) to one another and become one. God never intended for the union to be put asunder so another mate could be taken.

Malachi 2:14,16 – God hates divorce.

Romans 7:2,3 – Marriage is for life. A person, who is bound in marriage to a spouse, cannot have another companion as long as their first companion lives.

Matthew 19:3-9 (5:31,32) – What God has joined together, man must not put asunder. The only exception God allows, in which one may divorce a companion, is for the cause of fornication. If one divorces for any other reason, the divorce is a sin. And when he remarries he commits adultery. And whoever marries the one whom he put away commits adultery.

Applications

Never enter a Scripturally doubtful marriage.

1 Corinthians 7:10,11 – The only Scriptural alternatives for one who has improperly divorced are to remain unmarried or to be reconciled to his or her Scriptural spouse.

A divorced person should never remarry unless he is certain that he divorced his spouse because that spouse committed fornication. Before you remarry, search your soul and the facts of your case. Make sure your spouse was guilty of fornication and that was the reason why you divorced them.

Never marry a divorced person unless you are certain he or she obtained a divorce for Scriptural grounds. Have long talks and careful studies about the Bible teaching early in your relationship, before you develop strong emotions. Don't just take their word for it. Many divorced people deceive themselves or others in order to remarry. Talk to others who know the facts. Take the safe course and don't run risks with your soul.

When a divorced person remarries, his or her soul hangs in the balance, and so does the soul of the person he marries. If you really love someone, you will not endanger his or her soul or yours.

Enter marriage with a mutual determination to stay together for life.

Too many people enter marriage like they are buying a car: "I'll try this one, and if I get a lemon I'll just trade her in." Some even live together without marriage and call it a "trial marriage." They lack commitment. So, when problems arise, as they do in all relationships, instead of making a determined effort to work the problems out, they just end the marriage.

A "trial marriage" is not a marriage at all, because it does not involve a lifetime commitment. You can walk out anytime. That tells you nothing about marriage, because marriage involves commitment. That's why people, who do marry after living together, are more likely to divorce than those who do not live together before marriage. They think they have learned how to work together in marriage, but they haven't. They don't understand commitment.

When couples enter marriage with a true lifetime commitment, they will still face problems. But they will work together to solve the problems, because they are convicted that divorce is not an option. They must live together, so they need to work things out.

Furthermore, people who lack this commitment will not find their relationship ultimately satisfying. The beauty of marriage lies in knowing that you and another person value one another above all other people on earth, to the point that you are willing to commit yourselves to one another for life, no matter what the future holds. Only when you have that commitment will you find that, throughout life and even into old age, your marriage is truly satisfying.

The commitment of marriage is: "for better or for worse, for richer or for poorer, in sickness and in health, ***till death do us part***." That is not just tradition. It is not just a piece of paper. It is Bible principle ordained by Almighty God. Anything less fails to honor God or your spouse.

Young couples who are considering marriage need to have long, serious talks and Bible studies about the commitment of marriage. And they should never marry unless they are certain that they are both committed to stay married and be true to one another for life.

Maturity and Knowing One Another

Proverbs 5:1,2 – In advising his son about relationships with women, Solomon said to pay attention to wisdom and preserve discretion.

In some ways, whom you choose to marry is a matter of right or wrong (as when they are unscripturally divorced). Spiritual wisdom comes from God, but in many ways, the decision requires considerable judgment – not necessarily absolute rights or wrongs. I may not be able to prove everything I say here is Scriptural requirement, but I believe it to be good wisdom in harmony with Scripture.

Choose a Companion Based on Character, not Emotions.

Bible teaching

The Bible contains relatively few examples of choosing of marriage companions

Genesis 24 – Abraham's servant found a wife for Isaac. The couple never met till after the choice had been made. This specific choice was arranged by God (verses 50,51), which cannot happen today. But Abraham insisted that the bride come from among his relatives so he knew she did not come from the wicked people of the land. A man of wise judgment made the decision after entreating the blessing of God.

Genesis 29 – Jacob also went back to his mother's family to find a companion, because the young people where he lived were ungodly. He made his own decision that he wanted to marry Rachel after he had lived among her relatives for a month (verse 14). And even then, the agreement was that they would not marry till seven years later.

Ruth 2 – Ruth gleaned in the fields of Boaz throughout the length of the barley harvest and the wheat harvest. At the end of this period, they determined to marry. However, this too involved some differences from today. Ruth was a widow whose husband died without descendants. Boaz was a near kinsman of Ruth, and the law required him to take her as wife to raise up seed to her husband. But he knew her well by reputation. Her past life and conduct had been fully reported to him (2:11). She was known throughout the town as a virtuous woman (3:11).

But the Bible describes at length the character of godly wives and husbands.

The above examples involve some variation. But the one thing clear in every case is that what mattered most was the character of the one to be chosen. Many Scriptures describe the kind of person a man or woman must be in order to have a godly marriage.

Proverbs 31:10-31 – A virtuous woman is hard to find. Her character is described here and elsewhere. This is the kind of woman a young man should seek to find.

Likewise, the Bible describes the qualities of a godly husband. We will study these at length.

I know of no passage that states how you should *feel* toward a person before you marry them. You should love your spouse, but we will see that Bible love is more choice and commitment than emotion. Feelings are important in marriage; but if you marry a person of godly character, you can learn to love him/her. But a person of ungodly character will be a source of constant trouble to a Christian.

We will study the qualities of husbands and wives as we proceed. Before you marry you need to *know* – not just assume or even suspect – that your future spouse possesses these qualities. If not, either look elsewhere or give him/her time to change and prove they will be godly.

Applications

The entertainment industry bombards us with the romantic line to "just let your heart decide." Couples who have seriously different backgrounds meet, "fall in love," get married, and live happily ever after ... in the movies. Romantic, idealistic young women, with stars in their eyes, decide to marry guys with immoral backgrounds so they can reform them. This is foolish and incredibly dangerous.

Proverbs 28:26 – He who trusts in his own heart is a fool. ***Do not choose a spouse on the basis of feelings or instincts.***

A popular song years ago talked about a couple that met and married in the heat of passion, but they've been talking about divorce "ever since the fire went out."

Feelings come and go. You have highs and lows. People feel excited and high today, but tomorrow feel down and blue. This is normal for all people, even those who have good marriages. If you marry because a person excites you, you may regret the decision when the fire goes out.

Feelings come and go, but character should remain constant. Base your choice on character and you can sustain the relationship. Know one another well over a number of periods of emotional ups and downs, to see if your commitment can survive the downs as well as the ups.

Know One Another Very Well Before Committing to Marriage.

Ecclesiastes 5:2 – Do not be rash with your mouth, and let not your heart utter anything hastily before God. Marriage is a commitment before God. Do not enter it rashly.

In order to choose a companion based on character, it follows that you must know a person's character well in order to judge wisely.

Consider some specific applications.

Generally, you should know one another a long time.

We repeatedly taught our children to know a person for at least two years before they marry them – longer, if there were any significant questions about the person's character or spirituality. But the issue is not how long you know one another so much as how *well* you know one another. In some circumstances, people get to know one another more quickly than otherwise.

Someone says, "I know couples that got married a month after they met, and they had a good marriage." Yes, and I have heard of people who jumped out of airplanes without a good parachute and survived, but I still don't recommend it! And people who get married after a short courtship will not recommend it to their children! They ran a great risk, but were fortunate. For every such person, there are many who marry after a short acquaintance and live to regret it.

One of our daughters met a young man at college; and a few months later, they asked for our blessing on their wedding plans. But we did not know him and our first impressions were unfavorable. So, we stalled ... and stalled ... and stalled ... to get to know him better. After enough time passed, the young man revealed his true character, and our daughter broke off the relationship.

Proverbs 29:20 – Do you see a man hasty in his words? There is more hope for a fool than for him. Hasty commitment to marriage is absolutely foolish.

If you do not know a person well – well enough to put your life and even your eternal destiny on the outcome – then you are not ready to get married.

Growing a Godly Marriage

Talk about issues of importance in marriage.

Ask the other person his or her views about marriage, children, and especially about spiritual matters. Express your views and get their reaction. Study the Bible together. Learn your areas of agreement and disagreement.

And learn to work out your differences. Do not ignore your disagreements. Many people think their problems will just work out after marriage. How do you know? Usually they get worse! Discuss them now and see how well you are able to work out problems. Every marriage has problems. If you can't work out problems, you cannot succeed in marriage.

If you and your friend have not thoroughly discussed what you expect from marriage – and if you have not demonstrated your ability to resolve differences – you are not ready to marry.

Spend time together under many different circumstances.

Proverbs 23:7 – For as he thinks in his heart, so is he.

"Talk is cheap." Don't base your decision just on talk. Get to know a person's heart. The young man our daughter almost married said all the right things. But somehow his actions never seemed to accomplish his big plans.

Typical dating situations hide flaws. Couples put on their best behavior and best appearance to attract the other person. Friends and family may not tell you what they know about the person's shortcomings. **After** marriage is when all the character flaws become obvious – but it's too late. You need to know his or her character **before** marriage.

Karen and I often warn people about the danger of making a serious commitment when you've seen a person primarily in one setting, such as in the artificial environment of college, especially one like Florida College. Wait till you leave and see how your relationship survives.

Spend time together in various situations. Spend time with your family and friends. See how he treats his family and friends and how well he gets along with your family and friends. Go places where he or she likes to go and places where you like to go. Observe how he or she reacts under circumstances of stress, when things do not go as planned. Observe one another in the real world.

Consider a person's reputation and the judgment of godly family and friends.

Proverbs 15:22 – Without counsel, plans go awry; but in the multitude of counselors, they are established.

Boaz knew Ruth was a godly woman, because she had that reputation throughout the whole city. Sometimes a person's reputation – good or bad – is not deserved. But before you marry someone whose reputation is not good, make sure you know why he or she has that reputation.

Get to know well the family and friends of your potential spouse. Seek the honest evaluation of people who know the other person well and whose godly wisdom you trust.

The young man our daughter almost married was planning to preach. A preacher who knew them both well wrote a "letter of recommendation" to churches about him. About the only really good thing the letter said about the young man was that he wanted to marry a really outstanding young woman! The red flag was waving!

The opinions of others should not be final, but consider them carefully.

Both of You Should Be Old Enough to Make Mature Judgments.

1 Corinthians 14:20 – Do not be children in understanding; in malice be babes, but in understanding be mature.

Proverbs 7:7 – Describing a young man who lacked wisdom in his choice of women, Solomon said, "I perceived among the youths, A young man devoid of understanding."

Not all youths are foolish, but youths generally lack the mature judgment needed to make a wise marriage choice. Wisdom and good judgment come with age.

A choice of a marriage companion requires mature judgment.

Choosing a marriage companion is too serious to be made by immature people. The problem is that teenagers often tend to think they are much more mature than they are!

The divorce rate for people who marry in their teens is much higher than for people who marry in their twenties. Even people who marry in their early twenties are twice as likely to divorce as those who marry at 24-25 (*Focus on the Family*, 11/1992, p. 2).

Again, someone says, "I know people who got married in their late or even middle teens and had good marriages." Yes, but they will advise their children not to do it! And in most cases these were people who married years ago in a different age and different society when divorce was not easy like today. Often they worked things out, because society and their families frowned on breaking up marriage.

Marriage is one of the most important decisions you will ever make. If you follow the Bible, you will live the rest of your life with the person you choose. It is a choice you cannot change. It requires a mature decision. And maturity requires experience. And experience takes time.

Growing a Godly Marriage

Young people need experience with life and people before they make a choice.

Often young people are not settled regarding what they want in a spouse.

Observe older couples who have good marriages that have stood the test of time, and consider what kind of person you want to marry. Consider people whose marriages have failed and learn what kind of person you don't want to marry.

Get to know different kinds of young people, so you know what you're looking for. Visit with others, not just in dating situations, but also in groups, get-togethers, and family situations.

Our society encourages exclusiveness and intimacy early in relationships. Even young teenagers "go steady" – restrict dating to just one person. I urge parents and young people to resist that approach. We taught our kids they could not date at all till 16, and then only in groups or double dating. They could not single date till 18 and then only if we approved of the person.

Usually (though not always), people will have several relationships in various degrees of seriousness before they find one with whom to have a good marriage. I sometimes say I have never known anyone who found a good mate without first having their heart broken at least once.

You need to experience life's problems as well as its joys. If your parents are true Christians, chances are they have sheltered you from some of life's problems. That is a good thing. But it means you will need to be older before you are ready to make serious decisions like marriage.

Proverbs 20:25 – It is a snare for a man to devote rashly something as holy, and afterward to reconsider his vows. I can think of no area where this applies more than in marriage. Marriage is based on sacred vows. Entering those vows rashly and hastily generally leads to a snare. But after you are married, it is too late to reconsider your vows.

"Marry in haste, and repent in leisure." Studies confirm the wisdom of this. You will live with this person all the rest of your life, so why rush into it? Don't jump into exclusive relationships. And above all, don't jump into marriage. Take your time and make wise decisions.

If in doubt, **wait**! What do you have to lose by waiting, even another year or two? By taking your time to make sure of your choice, you have everything to gain and very little to lose.

Loving One Another

Ephesians 5:25,28,29 – Husbands should love their wives as Christ loved the church.

Titus 2:4 – Wives should love their husbands.

Love Is Concern for the Wellbeing of Others.

Bible Principles

Ephesians 5:25,28,29 – Jesus' love for the church illustrates the love husbands should have for their wives. He loved us so much He gave His life so we could be saved. So, the husband should be concerned for the wellbeing of the wife. He should nourish and cherish her as he does his own body. He must use his authority, not to please himself, but to do what is best for her and the family.

1 Corinthians 13:5 – Love is not selfish. (Romans 13:10)

Philippians 2:1-4 – Love requires us to not act from selfish ambition or conceit. We look out, not just for our own interests, but for the interests of those we love.

To have a good marriage, both spouses must seek the wellbeing of the other person. When one or both companions selfishly insist on their own way, problems are inevitable in the family.

Applications

Instead of love, couples often express self-will and lack of concern for their spouse.

Sometimes selfishness and lack of love shows in major ways.

The husband is lazy and won't work to provide for the family.

The wife is lazy and won't care for the house and children.

Growing a Godly Marriage

The husband spends money on toys he wants, but the wife and children lack clothes or food.

The wife prefers to socialize with her friends, leaving the house in a mess.

Sometimes lack of love shows in less obvious ways.

The husband treats his wife like a slave, but he won't lift a finger to get something for her. He sits in front of the TV saying, "I need a sandwich. Get me a Coke. How about some pretzels." But he would be furious if she made similar demands of him.

Or the wife has a list of work for the husband to do around the house, but gets mad when he watches TV. But while he goes to work, she watches TV, reads for pleasure, or visits with her friends for hours at a time, neglecting her own work.

Throughout our marriage, I have had all kinds of opinions about how Karen should dress to please me, but I used to get upset when she wanted me to dress to please her.

Love is a matter of degree and a matter of growth. But always, love seeks the wellbeing and pleasure of the other person, instead of just pleasing oneself.

Love Is a Choice of the Will.

Bible principles

Ephesians 5:25,28 – Love can be commanded, because it is a matter of the **will**. We can choose whether or not to love, just like we choose whether or not to obey any other command.

Romans 5:6-8 – Christ is the example to husbands. He loved us while we were yet sinners, not because we were so loveable He couldn't help Himself. He **chose** to do what we needed.

Titus 2:4 – Older women should admonish the young women to love their husbands, to love their children. Ladies can learn to love their husbands and children. Bible love is not primarily an emotion. It will result in emotions, but it itself results from the will.

Luke 6:27,28 – We are commanded to love our enemies. Loving one's enemy is about what it would take to put love into some marriages! But what does it mean to love an enemy? We do not uncontrollably "fall" in love. Rather, we **choose** to do what is best for them.

Love involves a **commitment**. It is not an accident. Love requires choosing to do what is best for one another. This takes deliberate effort. You do not just get married and automatically "live happily ever after." Such ideas make nice fairy tales – Cinderella and Snow White. But that's all they are: fairy tales!

Applications

Couples can learn to love one another.

Some think love just happens and cannot be controlled – you "fall in love" or out of love.

Sometimes one says, "I just don't love her/him any more." They may think nothing can be done except to get a divorce. But an appropriate response would be, "Have you repented? Have you confessed that sin to God and asked forgiveness?"

Lack of love does not excuse one from responsibility of marriage. It is a sin! What is the Bible solution to sin? Repent, confess it to God and to the one you sinned against. Then do right!

When a marriage lacks love, we choose whether or not to put it in!

When we realize we can **choose** to love, then we realize we **can put love into** a marriage. And if we fail to put it in, we **sin**.

Christ initiated love toward the church when we were sinners not acting lovingly toward Him. This is the example the husband should follow. Likewise, young women should be taught to love their husbands. You learn to love. If your marriage lacks it, you put it in.

This responsibility to initiate love rests on both spouses, specifically on the husband. Most people think the wife is responsible to put love in the marriage. She is responsible, but the husband is as much or more so. The command is emphasized to the man. He is to love the wife first and put love into the relationship, as Christ first loved the church.

Love Must Be Expressed in Both Word and Action.

The way to choose to love is to choose to say and do what is best for one's spouse.

Bible principles

Love should be expressed by what we say.

Ephesians 5:25 – Husbands should love as Christ loved the church. But Christ states His love for the church (Ephesians 5:2; John 3:16). So husbands and wives should express love for one another in words.

This does not require an overwhelming romantic "feeling" that wells up and can't help but be expressed. Remember, love is a choice of the will.

We choose to state: "I love you. I am committed to this marriage and to your welfare."

Love should be expressed by what we do.

1 John 5:2,3 – Love for others requires us to love God and keep His commands. Keeping God's commands is loving God.

1 John 3:18 – We must love, not just in words, but in deed and in truth. This is a vital principle in every home. We ought to say loving things, but that is not enough. We must act in love.
(Luke 10:25-37; 6:27,28)

Applications

Couples should show love in how they treat one another.

Other topics will emphasize the duty of husbands and wives in the home. The husband provides for the family and uses his authority for the good of the group. The wife keeps the home and submits in love to the husband. That is Biblical love.

Love is also shown in treating one another with respect. We speak respectfully. We show common politeness and decency. We consider one another's views.

Love for God and for our spouse must motivate obedience to all God's teachings about marriage. This is the basis of obedience to all Divine commands (Matthew 22:37-39).

Couples need to show love by being affectionate.

1 Corinthians 7:3 – You owe your spouse "affection" (NKJV). The emphasis is on sexual expression. But couples need to learn that sexual affection is just the culmination of other forms of affection. Without other forms of affection, sexual union is hollow, lacking beauty and meaning. When a couple is affectionate throughout the day, sexual affection has true beauty.

You say, "I'm just not an affectionate person. My parents were never affectionate, either." Then ***choose to change***! It may be harder for you, but love is a choice not a mood. You can change and become affectionate, just like you can change anything else necessary to please God.

This affection is "due" one another. It is not just an emotion or mood that overwhelms us, so we involuntarily start saying and doing sweet things. We should do and say kind things and express affection by ***choice***. Make a point to remember to say, "I love you" and to be intimate.

Don't' wait till some mood or force compels us. We can and should choose to act these ways.

Love Requires Giving and Self-Sacrifice.

Giving of self is the essence of love.

Bible principles

John 3:16 – God so loved the world that He ***gave*** His only-begotten Son.

Ephesians 5:25 – Jesus loved the church and ***gave*** Himself for it.

1 John 3:14-18 – If you see your brother in need and don't **give** what is needed, you don't have love.

Romans 12:20 – Loving you enemy requires **giving** food and drink when needed.

A fundamental requirement of a good marriage is a willingness to *give* of ourselves for the good of others.

The decision to act properly and lovingly toward our spouse should not depend on how our spouse acts, let alone how a mood hits us. We must choose to give of ourselves, because it is good for others and pleasing to God.

This is fundamental to being unselfish. Selfish people don't want to give in or sacrifice. They want to please themselves.

Giving and self-sacrifice is especially essential in solving conflict.

The fundamental lesson of Christ's love is to give up our own desires for the good of others, even when they are not acting the way we think they should.

In time of conflict, we say, "I'll do right or improve if he/she will too." If an act is beneficial for others, love requires us to **do it** regardless of what they are doing. If we have been wrong, love requires us to **admit it,** regardless of whether or not they have admitted their errors.

Even if we are convinced our spouse has caused a problem, we should ask ourselves honestly what we can do to help improve it.

This does not mean ignoring sin. Jesus did not cause our sin problem, and He did not compromise with sin. What He did was sacrifice Himself to provide a solution to the problem we caused. He did not just criticize our sin; He became involved to provide a solution. He did not do everything for us, but He made sure we had a way whereby we could overcome the problem.

A spouse may think, "He/she caused this problem, so let him/her solve it." Even if that is true, is it helpful? Instead think, "What can I offer to do – how can I become involved – so as to help resolve this problem?" Instead of saying, "Why don't you do this?" say, "Why don't you and I work on this **together**? What can I do to help?"

As long as neither spouse will take the first step toward a good marriage, the marriage can never be good. Each one must be committed to a good marriage. This requires us to give in at times where we wish we did not have to (assuming we do not sin). Each must be willing to sacrifice and give of themselves for the good of the marriage.

(1 John 4:9,19; Acts 20:35; Luke 10:25-37)

Growing a Godly Marriage

To improve your marriage, start with improving yourself.

If you are not married:

Make up your mind to marry only a person who will follow the Bible teaching about marriage. And then work to **become** the kind of person who will **attract the kind of person you want to marry**!

If you are a half-hearted Christian, halfheartedly involved in the church, practicing personal habits that are immoral or doubtful, do not expect to attract a faithful, dedicated Christian to marry! A dedicated Christian does not seek to marry a half-hearted Christian. To attract a faithful, dedicated Christian, you must **be** a faithful, dedicated Christian.

Likewise, if you have attitudes and habits that would hinder a good marriage, start now to change to become the kind of person who can work for a good marriage.

Likewise, if you are married:

If you are having problems in your marriage, do not expect your spouse to solve the problem. **Begin by examining yourself!** Most marriage problems result from faults on the part of **both** parties. Rarely is one person alone the whole cause of the problem.

1 Peter 3:1,2 – You cannot control what your spouse does. You can only control what you do. If you become what you should be, you will set the example to help your spouse become what he/she should be. Do not wait for them to change. Start doing all God says for you to do and you will have the best chance you can have for a good marriage.

Begin now to study the Bible teaching about the home, then conform your thoughts, words, and deed to that teaching. Become a faithful Christian and become the kind of person you need to be to have a Biblical marriage.

Differences we think we cannot tolerate should be resolved before marriage.

Some differences we may be able to live with. But if we know a person has a habit or characteristic that we find intolerable, especially if it is sinful, either resolve it before marriage or don't marry the person.

Do not marry a person thinking you will change them

Often girls meet guys with immoral habits or disgusting characteristics and decide to reform them. People say women can twist men around their little finger. And women believe it.

Or men think, since they are the head of the family, the wife will have to change to please them. But even without being head of the family, women can make your life miserable a thousand different ways.

If you are convinced your partner must change in order to have a happy marriage, then the time to make this known and resolve it is *before you marry them* – better yet, before you even become seriously emotionally attached. Once you are married, you are committed for life, and no amount of wishful thinking can change that (Romans 7:2,3).

If a person has serious *moral* problems, don't try to change them by *dating* them.

Explain what it is that troubles you, and encourage them to work with stronger, older Christians of their own gender. Then distance yourself from the relationship, till they prove they will change by their own choice. They must change, not because you want them to change, but because God requires it and changing is the right thing to do. Otherwise, they may go through the motions of change just to please you, then revert after marriage. Or, you may become so emotionally attached that you marry them despite the problem, and then live to regret it.

Learn to Love by Thinking, Speaking, and Acting for the Well-being of the Other Person.

How do you put love into a marriage where it is lacking? Instead of thinking first and foremost about what you want, act for their good and the good of your relationship. You choose to do what is best for the other person! That is Biblical love.

The key to putting love into marriage and keeping it in marriage is to do and keep doing the things that led you to love one another to begin with!

The reason couples stop loving one another is that they stop doing the things that led them to love one another! This is one of the most profound things I learned in 35 years of marriage. The incredible thing is that most of us are so foolish that we can't see that. This discussion involves a measure of judgment and wisdom, but it surely harmonizes with Bible principles.

How do couples learn to love in the first place?

Consider: What did you do that led you to decide that you loved one another and wanted to get married? We know how to put love into a relationship. We did it before we were married. We act a certain way to nourish love before marriage, then we get married and quit doing those things! If you want more love in your marriage now, go back and do the same things again!

Couples learn to love by saying and doing things to please the other person.

Before marriage, the young man sends the girl gifts, flowers, and cards. After marriage, he stops.

Before marriage, the young lady chooses her clothes, her perfume, and her hairstyle deliberately to please him. After marriage, she says,

"All my lady friends think this looks good on me. If he doesn't like it, something's wrong with him." Is that the way you thought before marriage?

Before marriage, you took the time to listen to her/him. After marriage, you don't have time.

Before marriage, did you show politeness and respect: hold the door for her, let her go first, and say "please" and "thank you"? Do you do those things now?

Before marriage, did you compliment her hair, her dress? Did you use expressions of affection? Why not now?

Before marriage, you remembered her birthday and other special days. What about now?

Before marriage, you went places and did things together. What about after marriage?

We know what cultivates love in a relationship. Why, after marriage, do we become brain dead? Go back and act the way you acted that led you into love. Don't wait for feelings or a special mood to strike you. Make a deliberate choice to do these things – love is a commitment.

Couples learn to love by taking time to be together.

Many times I have heard older couples say, "To keep love in a marriage you need to keep dating one another." For years that made little sense to me. Finally, I realized the point was that you **make appointments to spend time visiting together and doing things to please the other person**. That's how you learned to love, and that is how you stay in love!

Make an **appointment** once a week (at least once a month) to spend time primarily visiting with your spouse. And then once a year or so, take a few days to get away doing things together, talking, visiting, and just focusing on one another.

All of us live by some kind of schedule. We budget our time. Discuss your schedule with your spouse once a week (or at least once a month) and arrange an **appointment** for an evening or a couple of hours together. Do the things you did that led you into love.

We lose love, because we stop doing the things that produced love to begin with!

Many couples have excuses why they don't do these things.

* **"We don't have time."**

Did you have time before marriage? Why did you have time then, but not now? The answer is: You made the time, because it was important to you to be with her/him.

You have time to watch TV or visit on the phone with friends or read a book, etc. for 2-3 hours a week. But you can't spend that time with your spouse instead? What does that say?

Find someone to take the kids for an evening, trade babysitting with friends.

Make an appointment and don't break it except for absolute emergencies. If someone wants you to do something else say, "We have an appointment that evening."

* **"We can't afford it."**

You can't afford not to. Your marriage needs love. You must pay the price.

You don't have to spend a lot of money. Go for a walk in the park or the mall.

What did you do and where did you go before you got married. Do it and go there again!

The point is to spend time together.

* **"We don't enjoy the same things."**

She likes to shop; he can't stand to shop. He likes ball games; she can't stand ball games. Etc.

What did you do before you got married? You found things to do then! Do them again.

Then, you did not insist that your spouse do what you want. You did things she/he wants. Did you go shopping with her then? Did you go to ballgames with him then? Why not now?

Karen and I like to dress up and go out to eat, to a clean movie, or shopping. I don't much care to eat out. But I know she likes it. And I like seeing her look nice. We shop for something we both want to get; or we shop where she wants and then where I want.

The point is: If the object is to please the other person, to strengthen your relationship, and to show the other person you care, you find something to do and a way to do it, just like you did before you got married. Forget the excuses. You've already proved you can do it. Do it again.

What is missing in all these excuses? What is the fundamental problem?

When we make these excuses, we are saying we don't spend time together **because the other person and our relationship with that person are not important enough**!

If you don't have time or money for one another and don't' enjoy doing things together, how did you end up getting married? Before you got married, you found the time and the money and you found things to do. If you don't do it now, it's because your marriage relationship is not important enough. You don't *care* like you used to. We may not say it or think it, but our actions show it. And at least subconsciously, our spouse feels it. And that's why our marriages lack love!

Before marriage, you took time and money and you found things to do together, because you *cared* enough about one another. So, the

Growing a Godly Marriage

way to come to love one another again and to continue to love one another is to go back and do the things that led you to love one another to begin with.

Your marriage needs love. You have a command of God to put it in. Do what you did that led you to love to begin with.

Responsibility, Honesty, and Self-Control

Major marriage problems often are caused by irresponsible conduct, especially regarding honesty, financial matters, and uncontrolled temper.

Husbands and Wives Must Tell the Truth and Keep Their Promises.

God requires us to tell the truth.

Bible teaching

Proverbs 6:16-19 – There are 7 things God hates, and two of them involve lying and deceit: "a lying tongue," and "a false witness that tells lies."

Proverbs 30:8 – Remove far from me falsehood and lies. No servant of God wants a close relationship with one who practices lying or deceit.

Revelation 21:8,27; 22:14,15 – All liars will have their part in the lake of fire outside the holy city.

Ephesians 4:25 – Putting away lying, "Let each one of you speak truth with his neighbor," for we are members of one another. In no relationship is this truer than in marriage.

Romans 1:29,32 – Deceit is a twin brother of lying. It involves deliberately attempting to lead people to believe things that are not true. Those who practice it, and those who approve of others who practice it, both are worthy of death.

Psalm 40:4 – Do not have respect for those who turn aside to lies.

(John 8:44; Colossians 3:9; Psalm 24:3-5; 1 Peter 2:1,22; 3:10; Matthew 15:18-20; Proverbs 19:22; Exodus 20:16; Acts 5:1-9)

Growing a Godly Marriage

Applications

If we really understand this Bible teaching, why would we ever be dishonest with our marriage companion? Lying and deceit are always sinful. Why should we practice them toward those whom God has commanded us to love?

Marriage is based on mutual trust. When you sneak and deceive your spouse to get your way, you destroy the foundation of marriage and you sin against your spouse and against God.

And why would we marry anyone known to tell lies? If the person you are considering marrying lies to you or others, break off the relationship. A person who lies can never be trusted.

And if he/she lies to other people, don't think they won't lie to you. He will lie to anyone, when he thinks it is to his advantage. You never know when they are lying and when they are telling the truth. Why choose to live with that all your life?

God requires us to keep our promises.

Bible teaching

Hebrews 10:23 – God is faithful to His promises to us. This is just one of many characteristics God requires **us** to possess because it is a fundamental characteristic **He** possesses.

Genesis 29:18-28 – Laban agreed to give Rachel to Jacob for his wife if he would work seven years. But when the time came, he gave Leah instead. This is described as deceit (verse 25). Deceit characterized this whole family, and trouble repeatedly resulted. When a person can keep a promise but knowingly refuses to do so, that is deceitful. (31:4-13, 38-53)

Numbers 30:1,2 – The Lord commanded if a man vows a vow to the Lord, or swears an oath to bind himself by some agreement, he shall not break his word; he shall do according to all that proceeds out of his mouth. (Proverbs 22:25)

James 5:12 – Do not swear, either by heaven or by earth or with any other oath. But let your "Yes," be "Yes," and your "No," "No," lest you fall into judgment. (Matthew 5:33-37; 23:16-22; 2 Corinthians 1:15-20)

The fact we don't take oaths under the New Testament does not mean that keeping our word is less needed in the New Testament than in the Old Testament; rather, it is **more** necessary. In the New Testament, giving your word is binding, like Old Testament oaths were binding.

Romans 1:31,32 – Among those worthy of death are "covenant-breakers" (KJV & ASV). The NKJV says "untrustworthy" – surely, one who does keep his word is not trustworthy.

Matthew 7:12 (22:36-39) – The Golden Rule requires us to do to others as we want them to do to us. If it bothers you for people to make promises to you that they don't keep, then don't treat others this way.

(See also Proverbs 20:25; Ecclesiastes 5:2-6; Malachi 2:13-16; Jeremiah 34:8-22; Ezekiel 17:12-16; compare verses 17-21; Galatians 3:15; Josh 2:9-21; 6:22,23; 1 Kings 2:8,42,43.)

Applications

Sometimes extenuating circumstances might release us from a promise.

(1) We may have made a **conditional** promise. If the condition is not met, we are not obligated. (Sometimes conditions are understood, even if not stated.)

(2) Physical circumstances beyond our control may make it impossible to do as planned (like sickness keeping us from job, church meeting, etc.) (Luke 7:41,42; Matthew 18:24-34)

(3) The person to whom we made the commitment may agree to change the agreement (Proverbs 6:1-5; Luke 7:41,42; Matthew 18:24-34).

(4) If we committed ourselves to do something sinful, we must repent of having made the commitment, and then not keep it (Matthew 21:28-30).

But we must never make a promise that we have no intention of keeping. Having made a promise, we must not knowingly fail to keep it when we are able to keep it.

If a person does not honor his word and keep his promises, what reason do you have to believe he will keep the marriage vows? What evidence is there that he/she will stay with you till death or remain faithful sexually?

Few things do more harm to the marriage relationship than a partner who cannot be trusted to tell the truth and keep his/her word.

Husbands and Wives Should Pay Their Debts and Control Spending.

Money matters are one of the biggest causes of strife in marriage. Often the problem is caused by over-commitment to debt.

Bible principles

Christians must pay their debts.

2 Corinthians 8:21 – Provide for things that are honorable, not only in the sight of the Lord, but also in the sight of men. Being honorable in dealing with men requires paying our debts.

Psalm 37:21 – One who borrows and then does not pay again is wicked.

James 5:12 – Let your yea be yea and your nay, nay. If you don't intend to pay for a thing, don't promise that you will. If you do promise, then you are obligated to keep that commitment.

Romans 13:7,8 – Not only must we pay our taxes, but render to all what is due. This does not mean it is wrong to borrow. But when the payments come due, you must pay what you owe.

For Christians, there can be no doubt about whether or not debts will be paid. Failure to pay a debt is one form of dishonesty and failing to keep our promises.

(James 5:4)

One reason people are overwhelmed by debt is desire for material things.

Matthew 13:22 – In the parable of the sower, the thorny soil represents people in whom God's word is choked by the cares of this world and the deceitfulness of riches. These problems cause much marital strife and destroy marriages, as well as making people unfaithful to God.

1 John 2:15-17 – Do not love the world, or the things in the world. People are often led to buy things they cannot afford because of lust of the flesh, lust of the eyes, or pride of life. We see things that we think will satisfy our desires or that will make us feel important. We want what others have. But if we love the world, the love of God is not in us.

1 Timothy 6:6-10 – Those who desire to be rich fall into temptation and a snare, and into many foolish and harmful lusts. For the love of money is a root of all kinds of evil, for which some have strayed from the faith in their greediness, and pierced themselves through with many sorrows. Instead, we need to learn to be content with basic necessities.

Applications

Just because others have something doesn't mean your family needs it. Often a couple buys things they don't really need and can't really afford, then there is arguing about how the debts will be paid. Or both husband and wife work long hours to buy material things, but as a result they neglect their responsibilities to one another, to their children, to the church, etc.

Couples need to learn from the early days of their marriage to make a budget and live by it. Make a list of the things you need in order to live and how much each one will cost you. If you can't afford to pay for a thing and still spend the time and money you need with your family and in God's work, then learn to do without it.

Avoid debt whenever possible. Never make a debt unless you have every reason to believe you can pay it. If you make a debt, pay it.

If a person has demonstrated that they cannot control their spending and cannot learn to live on their income, then don't marry them. Or wait till they grow up and demonstrate in their life the basic honesty and self-control required to live within their means and pay their debts.

(Luke 12:15-22; Matthew 6:19-33)

Husbands and Wives Must Control Their Anger.

Bible teaching

Ephesians 4:26 – Being angry is not necessarily sinful, but we must control our anger or it will lead us into sin. (Mark 3:5)

James 1:19,20 – Be slow to speak, slow to wrath, because man's anger does not work God's righteousness. Learn not to get angry quickly, and do not speak quickly when you are angry. You can learn to control your temper. (Proverbs 14:17)

Proverbs 29:11,20 – A foolish man utters all his anger and is hasty in words. Sometimes people say, "I just say what I think," as though this justifies their sinful statements. But some things should not be thought, let alone said (Matthew 12:35-37). And wise men learn to control their speech. Only a foolish man says every thought that comes to his mind, especially when he is angry. (Ephesians 4:31,32; Proverbs 16:32; 25:28)

Proverbs 15:1,28 – When you are angry or your spouse is angry, study to answer (think about it carefully), and respond calmly.

Proverbs 22:24,25 – Make no friendship with an angry man, and with a furious man do not go, lest you learn his ways and set a snare for your soul.

Applications

Failure to control one's temper leads to sin and ruins many marriages.

Uncontrolled anger often leads to sin against others, especially those closest to us. It can even lead to violence and spouse or child abuse. If you have a temper problem, you must learn to control it if you ever expect to have a good home, to please God, or to receive eternal life.

If a person is known to have a bad temper that he often does not control, and especially if he is known to get violent, why marry him? Let him learn to grow up and prove he can control himself over a long period of time, or marry someone else.

You say, "He said he was sorry and asked me to forgive him."

Evil people often take advantage of the kindness of innocent people, especially young women. They lead you to believe that, if they say they are sorry, you must take them back and continue the relationship, even if you are not married.

Apologizing is good. But every liar will say he's sorry, when you catch him and prove unquestionably that he lied. People who frequently lose their temper will be sorry after they calm down. But real repentance requires changing, not just being sorry (Acts 26:20). Such characteristics are habits engrained in the character. They can be changed, but it will take time and motivation. Don't risk your soul and your happiness by marrying such a person.

If he apologizes and promises to change, you should forgive. But that does not require you to marry him or even to continue a relationship. Forgiving a person and marrying them are two different issues. Are you required to marry every person who asks your forgiveness? You are not required to marry anybody! You have every right to decide not to marry a person on any grounds you choose.

If he goes a year or two without committing such sins, you may have grounds to reconsider. But meanwhile, break off the relationship and let him prove himself willing to truly change. This keeps you free from an emotional bond that could bring you to ruin.

2 Peter 1:6; Galatians 5:22,23 – Self-control is both a fruit of the Spirit and a virtue one must add to his faith.

Before they marry, a man and a woman should both be mature and responsible enough to tell the truth, keep their promises, control their temper, and control their finances. If you are considering marrying a person who lacks self-control, do not think it will get better after marriage – it will probably get worse! Marry someone else, or at least wait until he/she grows up and enough time has passed to prove they have a pattern of responsible conduct.

If you are already married and have these problems, ***grow up***! Study the Bible and make a commitment before God to change. Then keep your word and change.

Friends and In-Laws

When you marry, you are marrying one person. But with him/her you "inherit" a whole new set of family members and friends. You will enter a close connection with his/her relatives and friends, and he/she will enter a relationship with your relatives and friends. Sometimes this leads to problems.

Sometimes There Will Be a Conflict with In-Laws and Friends.

Genesis 2:24 – When a man and woman marry, they form a new family separated from the families of either of their parents. The husband is to leave the parents and form a new and stronger tie with his wife.

Ephesians 5:22-25 – The new family has a head: the husband. Neither the man's parents nor the wife's parents are the head of this new family. Friends and family may make suggestions or give Biblical instruction or even rebuke when needed. But the husband is the leader of the new family, and his decisions should give primary consideration to the needs and wishes of his wife.

But some parents do not respect this and try to continue making decisions for their children as they have in the past. Sometimes the son or daughter has trouble "cutting the apron strings" and is too heavily influenced by his/her parents. The new husband may allow his parents to make decisions for him or may make choices on the basis of what pleases his parents instead of what meets the needs of his wife. Or the wife may seek to please or submit to her parents, instead of her husband. Such interference by family or friends may cause serious conflict in the new marriage.

Growing a Godly Marriage

Avoiding or solving this problem will take understanding of God's will and firm resolve on the part of the new couple. They must discuss the problem, preferably before marriage. Make sure you have a mutual understanding about what your relationship will be to family and friends. If you see evidence of a problem, discuss it. Then the new husband and wife must confront the troublesome family member, explain the Bible teaching, and take a firm stand.

Sometimes the only solution may be to move some distance away from the parents.

Your Companion Will Bring to the Marriage Habits and Attitudes Learned from His/Her Family and Friends.

Even if your mate's family or friends make no direct efforts to interfere in your marriage, your companion will come to the marriage with patterns of thinking, acting, and speaking that he/she developed from parents, relatives, and acquaintances. Observing his/her family and friends may help you understand him/her and know what to expect.

The effect of family influence

Ezekiel 16:44 – Like mother, like daughter. Or, as we sometimes say it, "Like father, like son." All of us our influenced by what we grew up with. We tend to continue to relate to people according to the habits we established growing up and according to the role models we observed.

1 Kings 15:3 – This and many similar verses describe people who were good or bad like their parents were. When children grow up with parents who have a good marriage, treat one another well, and are good parents, their children tend to act the same way in their marriage. But if the parents are alcoholic, abusive, or negligent, the children may act that way, even if they hated the way their parents acted. They lack a good role model to follow and may simply not know how to act differently.

It is possible to be different from what a person experienced while growing up, but this is difficult. If you do not like the way your future spouse's parents act in their home, or if you do not like the way your future spouse treats his family, then take care. It will be very difficult for your spouse to change these patterns, and you need to spend lots of time making sure he/she is determined and able to be different.

Nehemiah 13:23,24 – Both parents influence children. If you have conflict with your spouse's family, this needs to be dealt with thoroughly, preferably before marriage. If you marry this person, you will not only have to deal with their family themselves, you will also have to deal with their influence on your mate.

The effect of friends

Proverbs 13:20 – Companionship with fools will make us foolish, but association with wise men will make us wise. Christians realize that our associations, especially our closest companions, will have a major influence on the kind of life we lead. Evil companions corrupt our morals (1 Corinthians 15:33).

When you marry, you inherit your companion's friends. If you marry a person who has a habit of choosing bad companions or "running with a bad crowd," those people will become your companions too. If you marry a person who shows a pattern of wise choice of friends, then both of you will be able to associate with godly, moral people.

Proverbs 29:27 – An unjust man is an abomination to the righteous. But the ways of a righteous man are an abomination to the wicked! Before you marry a person, you need to consider how well you will get along with his friends and relatives and how well your spouse will get along with your family and friends.

Will your companion's friends and in-laws be the kind of people you will want to be visiting with frequently, especially after you have children? Does the person you are considering marrying make wise choice of his/her closest friends? And how will your spouse react to your family and friends?

Discuss these matters carefully before marriage and after marriage. Determine to marry a person only if he/she shows a commitment to good relationships and good influences. After marriage, continue to study God's word together and reevaluate the influence your family and friends have on you, on your marriage, and on your children.

Growing a Godly Marriage

Roles of Husband and Wife

Traditionally and Biblically, the roles of husband and wife were fairly well defined. God created men and women different and assigned them different roles.

Modern philosophies, however, pressure modern families to believe these roles will not work in modern society. Indeed, they may not work – if we want to have the kind of families people in the world have. But if our primary goal in marriage is to serve God, then we will find the roles defined in the Bible are the *only* ones that will work!

Biblical roles require the following:

The Wife Must Submit to Her Husband, But He Must Rule with Love.

The Bible teaches wives to submit to their husbands.

Genesis 3:16 – God decreed that the man should rule over his wife. This is neither the invention of men nor the product of evolution. It is a decree of Almighty God.

Ephesians 5:22-25 – The wife should submit to her husband as the church should submit to Christ. And, she must submit in "everything." She has no more right to pick and choose which decisions she finds acceptable or reasonable, than the church does regarding Jesus' decisions. The only exception is if her husband tells her to do something that would be sinful to do; then she "must obey God rather than men" (Acts 5:29).

Further, the church should cooperate with Jesus' authority in every way possible, submitting willingly out of love (John 14:15). Likewise, the wife should not try to look for loopholes or sneak behind her husband's back or manipulate his decisions by devious means. The command to love her husband (Titus 2:4) should lead her to seek to know his will so she can obey it.

1 Peter 3:1-7 – If her husband is disobedient to God and even if he misuses his authority, even then the wife is not justified in refusing to submit. In fact, this just gives more reason why she should submit, so she can set him a good example. (Compare Romans 12:17-21.)

(See also Colossians 3:18; Titus 2:5; 1 Corinthians 11:3,8-12.)

The Bible teaches husbands to use their authority with love.

Ephesians 5:25-29,33 – While the husband is head of the wife, he must also rule with love as Jesus does for the church.

A man who loves his wife will not use his authority just to get his own way and please himself. Instead, he will rule for the good of all (1 Corinthians 13:5). This often requires him to sacrifice his own desires for the good of the group, even as Jesus did in dying for the church.

Further, the husband should make a reasonable effort to consult his wife in decisions that affect her; he should take her will into consideration. God grants the church the right to influence His decisions by our prayers. For a husband to refuse to do this would be failing to love his wife as himself: you would not like people to make major decisions that affect you without your input. Likewise, using family funds to do as you please, without careful consideration of the wife's needs and views, is selfish and unloving.

This does not mean the husband always does what the wife wants. He does what he honestly concludes is best; but making good decisions requires a willingness to receive input from those who must follow the decisions.

Again, Jesus acted with love for the church, even when we were in sin (Romans 5:6-10). Likewise, the husband must not be unloving toward his wife, even when she is disrespectful or even sinful. On the contrary, he must seek to put love in the home, even when the wife is unloving, just as Jesus did for the church.

1 Peter 3:7 – The husband should strive to *understand* the needs of the wife and value her, so that he can make his decisions accordingly.

He should honor her (compare cherish – Ephesians 5:29). The wife should not to be treated as property or a slave, but as a valued and respected companion.

The fact the husband is the leader does not mean the wife is any less valuable or important. In God's plan, value and importance are not determined by authority, but by the service we perform (Matthew 20:20-28). Men and women were each uniquely created by God to fill the role He planned for them. Though their authority and abilities differ, each is equally valuable and important in his/her role (compare 1 Corinthians 12:14-22).

Young people, do not marry someone unless you are truly convinced that he/she will practice Biblical roles. Young lady, God will require you to submit to your husband for the rest of your life, even when you don't like his decisions and even if you think he is unreasonable. The marriage commitment must be to "love, honor, and **obey**." Consider that carefully long before you say, "I do."

Young man, God will require you to love your wife and make decisions for her good without bitterness, even when you think she is not submitting to you properly. When you choose a marriage companion, choose someone whose example and conduct indicates understanding of Bible roles and commitment to follow them.

This is another reason why it is so important to really take your time and be sure you know a person well before you marry.

The Husband Is Responsible to Provide Family Income and the Wife Is Responsible to Be the Homemaker.

The Bible often states the husband's responsibility to provide family income.

Genesis 3:17-19 – From the beginning the man was responsible to labor with his hands to provide bread A man who is able to do this but will not, is lazy and foolish (Proverbs 24:30-34). (1 Thessalonians 4:10-12; 2 Thessalonians 3:10)

Ephesians 5:28-31 – The man should labor, not just to provide for himself, but also to "nourish and cherish" his wife as he does his own body. These terms include providing and caring for her, as well as protecting her. (Compare verse 23.)

1 Timothy 5:8 – The man who will not provide for his own, especially his own household, is worse than an unbeliever. Yet, all across the country there are men who fail to provide for their families as they ought. Even though they are able-bodied, they live off welfare or off relatives or institutions. Meantime, their families suffer.

The Bible is filled with examples of men who were employed in various occupations by which they provided for their families, including occupations that often took them away from their families through the day. This includes sailors, shepherds, physicians, tax collectors, carpenters, fishermen, preachers, etc. There is no passage, however, that teaches wives, especially if they are mothers, that they are similarly obligated to leave their families and work to provide income.

Mothers are instructed to be homemakers, managing the home.

Bible teaching

Genesis 2:18ff – The wife was created to be a companion and helper to her husband. She finds her fulfillment, not in competing with the husband in his work nor in taking his responsibilities, but in assisting him. (Titus 2:4)

1 Timothy 5:14 – She should manage the household. (Compare Proverbs 31:27.)

Titus 2:5 – She should be taught by the older women to be a homemaker (NKJV; "worker at home" – ASV).

Psalm 113:9 – She should rejoice and praise God for her role as mother and keeper of a home. Husbands ought to praise their wives for fulfilling this role.

Proverbs 7:11,12 – It is a shame for a woman to gad about instead of staying at home.

John 10:11-14 – Some work cannot be done by one who is simply hired, as well as it can be done by one who has a personal relationship. What is true of caring for mere animals would surely also be true of caring for our family members. Ladies, no one can love and care for your husbands and your children like you can. Can you hire another woman to fulfill your role as companion to your husband and submit to him in your place? Then why think your can hire a day-care center, babysitter, or other hireling to love and care for your children in your place?

Applications

The roles of wife, mother, and homemaker are not the only responsibilities God requires of women. He also requires them to teach His word, be active in the church, care for the needy, visit the sick, and be diligent in prayer and Bible study, etc. Some of these activities may even briefly take her away from her house. But it should be clear that filling all her God-given roles would constitute a full-time job for any mother.

The Bible simply does not approve of the idea of modern society that family roles are to be shared equally or interchanged or hired out to others. Most of the major problems that exist in modern homes can be traced to a failure of husband, wife, or both to understand and properly fill their God-given role.

There may be circumstances in which the husband or wife is unable to do their work, so their spouse may take the duties of a companion in an emergency circumstance. And wives may find ways to contribute to family income without leaving their children or neglecting their families or their homes. But the fact remains that God said the man is responsible to be the head of the family and the one to provide

Growing a Godly Marriage

the income, and he said that the woman is to be in subjection and is to be the homemaker. Yet, all across the country there are families in deep trouble because husbands and/or wives neglect their God-given duties because they spend so much time doing things other than what God requires them to do.

Young lady, make sure you marry a young man who is willing and able to provide for you and the family. If he doesn't hold down a job or doesn't show clear evidence of being able to provide an adequate living, or if he might encourage or even expect you to work so you cannot stay home and be a mother to your children, you need to resolve this before marriage. And while you should prepare to provide for yourself if you cannot find the right young man to marry, nevertheless you need to organize your education and lifestyle so that, when the right man does come along, you are prepared and willing to be a fulltime homemaker.

Young men, you make sure that the young woman you marry is committed to staying home and being a fulltime mother to your children. If she is career-minded or expects a lifestyle that you can't provide, make a serious effort to resolve this before marriage.

And throughout marriage, avoid making financial commitments that require two incomes. Some couples, early in marriage, develop commitments and attitudes that encourage the wife to continue working outside the home even after the children come. The best way to avoid these problems is to never put yourselves in the situation where you must have two incomes to make ends meet.

Sexual Purity

Our son-in-law Brian teaches junior high school in a rural district of a conservative state. Students in class brought up an eighth-grade boy, who had been expelled for bad behavior, then fathered a child out of wedlock. The majority of students believed he would be a good father. Brian said he should have waited till he was married. The class responded that everyone has sexual relations before marriage; no one waits! They expressed disbelief when he said he had waited and had never been divorced. When he said couples should work hard to have a good marriage, they could not understand why!

When young people have been taught they evolved from animals, why should they reserve the sexual union for marriage or view marriage as a lifetime commitment? Animals see no need for such things.

When even homosexuals can marry, marriage must not mean much. *World* reported a study at the Hoover Institute: "Scandinavian gay marriage has driven home the message that marriage itself is outdated and that virtually any family form, including out-of-wedlock parenthood, is acceptable ... in Sweden, the few young couples who do get married often do not like to admit it, since what they have done is so far out of the norm that they feel embarrassed."

The public media virtually refuses to even acknowledge marriage. It is politically incorrect to even mention words like "husband," "wife," or even "spouse." Instead, the media continually refers to your "partner," "companion," or "significant other." And "family" has been redefined to describe any group of people who live together and care for one another in some way.

No wonder young people do not respect the importance of marriage or of reserving the sexual union for marriage.

Reasons for Reserving the Sexual Union for Marriage.

Consider reasons why Christians should respect marriage as a lifetime commitment between one man and one woman, and specifically why the sexual union should be reserved only for marriage.

Marriage was created by God and is "very good."

Genesis 2:18-24 – At creation, God observed that it was not "good" for man to be alone, so He created woman and ordained marriage. Within marriage, a **man** cleaves to his **wife** and they become one flesh (which includes the sexual union – 1 Corinthians 6:16).

Note that animals were not adequate, nor did God create another man as a mate for man. He created a woman as a companion for man. So, God ordained marriage and the sexual union within marriage. God declared this to be "good." It meets a fundamental need. In fact, everything God made at creation was "very good" (Genesis 1:31).

Those who believe in God, and specifically in God as Creator, must believe that marriage is "good" and is the relationship ordained of God for the sexual union.

God's word forbids sexual relationships outside marriage.

Hebrews 13:4 – Marriage is honorable and the sexual relationship (the "bed") is undefiled only within marriage. Note that the sexual union is not inherently evil. But the passage defines "fornication" and "adultery" to be sexual union ("the bed") outside marriage. God will judge such conduct.

Exodus 20:14 – The Old Testament commanded to not commit adultery.

Mark 7:20-23 – Jesus taught that fornication comes from the heart and defiles a man.

1 Corinthians 6:9-11 – The Corinthians had been fornicators, adulterers, homosexuals, etc. Those who practice this cannot inherit the kingdom of God.

1 Corinthians 6:16-18 – Fornication is wrong because it constitutes being "one flesh" with someone other than one's lawful spouse. This refers back to God's plan, which places the sexual union in marriage (Genesis 2:24).

Revelation 21:8; 22:14,15 – Fornicators are among those who will not enter heaven but will be in the lake of fire.

1 Corinthians 7:2-4 – To avoid **fornication**, one should satisfy the sexual desire only with "his own wife" or "husband." God expressly confirms that marriage companions must be of the opposite gender and that each may satisfy sexual desires only with his/her marital companion.

So, marriage is the authorized relationship for satisfying the need for lifetime companionship and for sexual affection. But it involves one man with one woman with a lifetime commitment. Only that relationship is honorable by God's decree.

God says sexual relations before or outside marriage are wrong, no matter how much we care for the other person. These passages should settle the issue. But sometimes God gives additional reasons for His decrees. Consider additional reasons He gives for saving ourselves for our marriage companion.

(Ephesians 5:3-5; Galatians 5:19-21; Colossians 3:5-10; 1 Timothy 1:9-11; Proverbs 5:1-23; 6:23-7:27; 1 Thessalonians 4:3-8; 1 Corinthians 5:9,10; Ezekiel 16:32)

Sexual acts outside marriage lead to jealousy, alienation, violence, and disease.

Proverbs 5:1-18 – Relations with an immoral woman lead to bitterness (verse 4), dishonor (verse 9), poverty (verse 10), grief (verse 11), destruction of flesh and body (verse 11 – as in sexually transmitted diseases), and even death (verse 5). All of us have heard of people who have experienced some or all of these as a result of sexual promiscuity.

People think venereal diseases can be avoided by "safe sex" or cured by modern medicine. If so, why are many such diseases at all-time highs? And why do we continually hear about the dangers of AIDS? Despite politically correct views, the fact is that AIDS is essentially a sexually transmitted disease. Those who avoid illicit sex and illegal drugs have little need for concern.

The solution: stay far away from those who are sexually promiscuous (verse 8), and rejoice with the wife of your youth (verses 15-18).

Proverbs 6:32-35 – Adultery leads to wounds, dishonor, and reproach. It causes jealousy, fury, and vengeance, which cannot be appeased. This occurs when people violate marriage vows, but it also occurs among people in trial marriages and homosexual relationships. (7:21-27)

Such conduct often brings a burden of guilt to a relationship, which manifests itself in many ways. We may be angry for no apparent reason or unable to express affection freely. When we know our spouse has done this outside marriage (even if they did it with us), we may wonder if he/she will do it again, or with how many others they have done it.

Matthew 19:9 – Sexual union outside marriage is so serious that it is the only grounds for which God will permit the one who is pure to divorce and remarry.

When people practice chastity before marriage and sexual faithfulness in marriage, they need not be concerned about the problems caused by promiscuity. There are reasons why God has restricted the sexual union to marriage. Obeying his plan is always best.

Marital commitment provides a stable relationship for raising children.

Genesis 1:26-28; 2:24 – God created male and female, told them to have children (reproduce), and said man should be "one flesh" with his wife. One reason God restricted the sexual union to marriage is that this gives children **a family with both a father and a mother to raise them**.

Proverbs 1:8 – Children should hear the instructions of their father and not forsake the law of their mother.

The fundamental concept throughout Scripture is that children should be raised in a family consisting of a father and mother who train and provide for them (Ephesians 6:2-4; Luke 2:48-51; Genesis 4:1,25; etc.). Marriage, with a lifetime commitment of husband and wife, provides the stable, loving relationship that children need.

Sometimes circumstances beyond our control take away father or mother, but these should be viewed as tragedies. **Any relationship, which runs the risk of conceiving a child without the benefit of both a father and a mother to raise it, is irresponsible, unloving, and immoral.**

Since the sexual union is the means God designed to conceive children, it follows that having this union outside of marriage can and often does result in children born out of wedlock. Such conduct is irresponsible, unloving, and immoral. Yet, significant portions of children today are born out of wedlock. No child should ever have to fear that his parents would choose to risk his being born or raised in such an immoral, irresponsible circumstance.

Marital commitment provides the needs of old age.

Because marriage is a lifetime commitment, it provides a permanent relationship of companionship and love, even into old age.

Romans 7:2,3 – Husband and wife are bound to one another as long as they live. Those who are true to their marriage vows, will have a spouse to live with, until death parts them. Few things in life are more beautiful than a couple that continues to love and care for one another into their older years.

Young people, who choose promiscuous or homosexual relationships, have no such companionship. They may pass from partner to partner, living for the moment, with no thought of the consequences for old age. Likewise, people who divorce without Scriptural cause, have no right to a companion in their older years. People, who are not true to their marriage commitment, have no reason to expect others to be committed to them.

Likewise, parents who raise children in a committed family, will have children to care for them in their older years.

Ephesians 6:2,3 – Honoring parents includes caring for them in their old age.

1 Timothy 5:4,8,16 – When parents become elderly, especially when they are widowed and their marriage companion is gone, their children should see that their needs are met. (Compare Matthew 15:4-6; Ruth 4:13-15; John 19:25-27.)

This is called "repaying" the parents. But if parents bring children into the world without a committed family relationship with both a father and a mother to love and care for them, what reason do children have to be committed to them in their old age? If such children learn to care for their parents, it won't be because the parents set a good example of caring for them.

The true beauty of the sexual affection is experienced only in true marriage.

1 Corinthians 7:2-5 – To avoid fornication, man and woman should marry and then should give one another the **affection** that is **due**. You do not have authority over your own body to enjoy this affection, except with your committed marriage spouse.

In a committed marriage, the sexual union becomes the ultimate expression of affection, love, and companionship. By reserving this relationship only for our lawful spouse, we are telling them, "I love you so much that I have chosen you to be the only person in the world in which I will engage in this most intimate expression of love." This makes sexual affection the incredibly special bond of love that God intended it to be.

Surveys have repeatedly shown that couples who remain true to their marriage commitment express much greater satisfaction with sexual affection.

Like everything else that God created for good, when people pervert it, they cannot fully enjoy its benefits. People, who practice casual, recreational sexual activities, will never, ever enjoy the true beauty of sexual affection, and most will never even understand what they missed. The brief, passing pleasure such people enjoy can never measure up to committed marital bliss.

Applications of Sexual Purity

Obviously, there are limits to what can properly be discussed in a public forum. Bible teachers have a problem because, if they give detailed discussion, some object that they are too explicit. But if we are not specific enough, many young people will get in trouble because no one warned them what guidelines and limits they should respect. We need to be as explicit as the Bible and specific enough to properly apply Bible teaching.

Avoid tempting circumstances and conduct before and after marriage.

Proverbs 5:8; 6:26-29 – The point of Solomon's warnings was to stay away from people and circumstances that would seduce you to violate sexual purity. Don't make close friendships with people who are promiscuous, and don't participate in tempting activities. (7:6-27)

Proverbs 6:23-25; Matthew 5:27,28 – The way to avoid immoral conduct is by keeping your thoughts pure. Avoid the lustful thoughts that lead to immoral conduct. And the way to avoid the lustful thoughts is to avoid conduct that leads to lustful thoughts (sexually suggestive flirting).

Titus 2:5 – Young women should be taught to be "chaste" – virtuous, modest, not indecent. This applies to clothing, words, and conduct. (2 Corinthians 11:2; Philippians 4:8; Luke 8:27,35; 1 Timothy 2:9,10; 2 Samuel 11:2-4)

Romans 13:13,14; Mark 7:20-23; Galatians 5:19-21; 1 Peter 4:1-4 – God forbids "lascivious" or "licentious" conduct – anything that causes or tends to arouse sexual excitement, desire, or lust between people not married to one another.

Young men and women need to be taught that there are ways of speaking, dressing, and acting that arouse sexual desire. These are good and proper in marriage, because married couples can properly act on those desires. But when you have no right to fulfill the desire, then you have no right to arouse it in yourself or in one whom you are courting.

Young people, when you are dating, make sure both you and your date keep your hands off areas that should be reserved for marriage. Make sure you keep clothing on and cover what only married people have the right to see. Don't date anyone who doesn't understand these principles or that has a reputation for improper conduct. At the first sign of improper conduct, stop and insist on respect for purity. If you need more specific guidance, get advice from your parents or from respected older Christians (Titus 2:4,5).

Likewise, married people should avoid the dangers of forming too close relationships with people of the opposite gender other than your spouse. Avoid the very appearance of a "dating" situation. Avoid being alone in private. At the first sign of improper conduct, immediately distance yourself from the friendship.

And don't think nothing wrong can happen, because you are both Christians. Even faithful Christians have been brought to sin by forming too close friendships with people of the opposite gender. Often the relationship begins because we have a special relationship with other Christians, we think we are safe so we drop our barriers, and soon we have an illicit relationship.

"***Flee*** fornication."

(Proverbs 4:23; 6:27; 13:20; 22:3; Matthew 5:8; 6:13; 18:8,9; Romans 13:14; 1 Corinthians 15:33; Genesis 39:7-12)

Spouses should express sexual affection in marriage.

1 Corinthians 7:2-5 – With your true marital spouse you not only may be intimate, but you should do so freely. You and your spouse have no one else with whom to fulfill this desire. Be free and expressive of your affection.

Verse 5 – Failure to do this allows Satan to tempt us to a lack of self-control. This can happen when one withholds affection in anger or in an attempt to punish the other. Or it can happen because of prolonged physical separation. Avoid either form of temptation.

Verses 3,4 – Both the husband and the wife are to show affection; neither is to deprive the other (verse 5). This is not just for the husband's pleasure. Both will truly be blessed provided both truly seek to show affection.

Remember that sexual affection is an expression of love. As we discussed previously, love requires **giving to please the other person**. Love is destroyed by selfishness. Nowhere is that true more than in sexual affection. Your relationship will be blessed to the extent that you set aside what you want and try to please your companion. Both spouses – but especially husbands – need to be patient, gentle, and giving. **The most basic thing to remember about sexual affection in marriage is that it is an expression of love and should always be guided by a genuine desire to please the other person.**

One writer referred to proper sexual affection in marriage as "the twenty-year warm up." At first, you are not sure how to please one another. It may even help if, shortly before or soon after marriage, you personally read a wholesome, helpful book. But as you truly seek to please one another, you will grow in understanding throughout your marriage.

And that's another reason why people will never fully enjoy the blessings of sexual affection, if they don't appreciate marriage. A married couple, who truly love one another, will grow in affection over long periods of time. People who lack marital commitment are generally selfish in their approach and won't take time to grow. Their acts are expressions of lust and selfish desires, rather than true love and commitment.

Conclusion

As society declines, those who have left God's word will grow worse and worse in their perversions of marriage and the sexual relationship. But those who seek to truly be blessed in this life and in eternity need to learn to appreciate and obey God's plan for marriage.

God has created many incredibly powerful forces. When those forces are used improperly, they can do incredible harm. When used properly, they can be incredible blessings. Nothing destroys a relationship between a man and woman more totally that sexual immorality. But proper affection in marriage makes it the true blessing of companionship that only God can design.

Solving Marriage Conflict

Introduction

Every family has disagreements.

Someone once told about a couple celebrating many years of marriage. The man said, "I'm pleased to say that we've never had a fight." The wife responded, "Well, it helps to become old and forgetful!"

There is no such thing as a couple that never has conflicts. Unfortunately, many couples lack the **skill** to discuss their disagreements and **resolve** them. As a result, conflicts may lead to *fighting,* in which the **husband and wife become seriously alienated but never resolve the cause of the problem.** Instead, they build up bitterness, quarreling, uncontrolled anger, hatred, and often divorce.

The purpose of this study is to learn what the Bible says about how to resolve conflict in marriage.

We are concerned with conflict in general, but especially with **serious** conflicts that destroy the relationship of husband and wife and that may lead to divorce.

Specifically, couples need the ability to discuss serious problems, reach a plan to resolve them, and then put that plan into action. I emphasize that this is a **skill** that many people have simply never learned, but which **can be learned**. We hope to learn what the Bible says about how to develop this skill.

Consider the following steps that can help couples avoid or resolve such serious problems.

Growing a Godly Marriage

Trust in God

Believe that God Can Help Your Marriage.

Many couples have bickered and quarreled so long that they lose hope things will ever improve. They resign themselves to go on quarreling and hating the rest of their lives, or they end the marriage by divorce.

Philippians 4:13 – I can do all things through Christ who strengthens me. If we trust in ourselves, we may fail. But we must believe that Jesus will provide the strength we need to please God.

1 John 5:4 – If we are born of God, we overcome the world through *faith*. This includes overcoming improper family relations, but we must *believe* that it can be done by the power of God.

Couples need to believe that, by God's power, they *can* resolve their marriage problems if both parties will really work at it.

Pray for God's Help.

Philippians 4:6,7 – Don't be anxious, but by prayer and supplication make your requests known to God. Christians should do this for all our problems, but specifically for our marriage problems. If we have proper *faith* in God's power, then we will pray diligently about our marriage problems.

1 John 5:14 – Be confident that, if we ask according to His will, He hears us. (Matthew 6:13; 1 Peter 5:7)

When we have marriage problems, especially serious ones, we need to believe that God will answer prayer. If both the husband and wife are faithful Christians then, both individually and together, they should spend much time praying for God's help with their problems. Confess your problems specifically and ask God's help.

But remember that God answers according to His will. If your companion is not a Christian or is not faithful, God will not *force* him/her to do right. He may, however, give them an opportunity to learn His will for their lives.

When your family faces serious problems, how much do you pray to God and trust His power to answer your prayers?

Respect Bible Authority.

Follow Bible teaching instead of feelings, human wisdom, etc.

Proverbs 3:5,6 – Trust in the Lord and let *Him* guide your path. Don't lean on your own human understanding. Too often troubled couples seek sources of guidance outside the Bible.

Some folks follow psychologists, marriage counselors, advice of friends, etc. Sometimes such sources may help if their advice agrees with Scripture. But they usually offer human wisdom instead of Scripture.

Other couples are guided by *feelings*. People get divorced saying, "I just don't *feel* anything for her (or him) anymore." But no amount of feelings can change what God's word says.

2 Timothy 3:16,17 – Scriptures provide to *all* good works. If solving marriage conflict is a good work, then the Bible will tell us how to do it. Other people may help, but we must reject any ideas that do not agree with the Bible.

Many people accept this view of authority regarding salvation, worship, church organization, etc. Why should it be any different regarding our homes?

(2 Peter 1:3; Jeremiah 10:23; Proverbs 14:12; etc.)

Study what the Bible says about your problem.

Psalm 1:2 – The righteous man delights in God's law and meditates on it day and night. If we really believe the Bible has the answers, then we should study what it says. This is what we would do about any other spiritual problem. Why do otherwise regarding family problems?

Acts 17:11 – The Bereans learned the truth by searching the Scriptures day and night. We need to do the same regarding our family problems.

Then Obey the Bible Teaching.

Matthew 7:24-27 – The wise man not only hears what God's word says, but also *does* it. The foolish man hears but does not obey.

If we believe that God's word holds the answers to our marriage problems, then we must determine to *do* what it says, not just *learn* what it says.

Growing a Godly Marriage

Hatred, bitter quarreling, and alienation in our homes mean that someone is disobeying God.

God created marriage for the **good** of man and woman. He never intended for marriage to be a source of hatred and bitter grudges. It follows that serious marriage conflict is not God's will for us.

Serious marriage problems either began because someone disobeyed God, or else the original problem led someone to commit other sinful acts. In either case, **serious marriage problems almost always involve sin.**

If so, then we can overcome the problems by the same methods the Bible describes for overcoming other sins! **Recognizing that sin is the root of the problem gives hope, because a Christian knows that God has the solution to sin.**

However, marriage involves **two** people. A problem between two people can only be completely removed if **both** parties are willing to work at it. If only one person obeys God, the other person can keep the problem alive.

Nevertheless, if your spouse will not work to improve the marriage, this does not remove your responsibility to do what you can.

To please God, **you** must follow His will regardless of what your partner does. You must believe that **you** can please God regardless of how others act.

If both parties commit themselves to practice God's plan, any couple can eliminate sin from their marriage. And regardless of whether or not your partner obeys God, **you** can still please God if you will follow the steps we are about to describe.

(1 Corinthians 10:13; 2 Corinthians 9:8; Joshua 1:5-9; Ephesians 3:20,21)

Respect God's Pattern for Marriage.

As we study God's word, we will learn that He has a pattern for marriage.

God Has a Pattern for the Permanence of Marriage.

Divorce and separation are not acceptable options.

Romans 7:2,3 – Marriage is a lifetime commitment.

Matthew 19:9 – One can Scripturally divorce a spouse only if it is done because he/she has committed fornication. Obviously one should never want his/her spouse to commit fornication, so it follows that each one must sincerely hope for the marriage to continue. (Matthew 5:31,32)

1 Corinthians 7:10,11 – If we have unscripturally divorced, we must seek reconciliation with our spouse or remain unmarried. Remarriage is not an option.

1 Corinthians 7:2-5 – Since the sexual union is upright only within marriage (Hebrews 13:4), the man and wife should fulfill one another's desires for sexual affection. They should not voluntarily separate except by mutual consent for a temporary time for spiritual purposes.

Sometimes troubled couples choose to live apart, thinking they will not divorce. But separation causes sexual temptation, and it weakens commitment to the marriage and increases the likelihood of divorce. Doubts about one another's conduct and motives increase. Problems cannot be discussed and resolved because you are not together.

The Bible requires both spouses to continually view the marriage with commitment.

Growing a Godly Marriage

Both spouses should express commitment to the marriage.

Sometimes one will make statements and threats that express lack of commitment to the marriage.

One may say:

"I wish I never married you." You are bound for life. What good comes from such a statement?

"I should have divorced you years ago."

"If this doesn't stop, I'll see a lawyer."

"I'm leaving, and I don't know if I'll be back."

In the absence of Scriptural grounds for divorce, all such statements are ***sinful***, because they destroy the security and commitment of the marriage. They do not express love, but are used as a weapon to threaten and hurt the spouse.

It is sinful, not just to practice wrong, but also to *desire* or to *threaten* to do wrong.

If it is wrong to do a thing, then it is wrong to desire to do it or to threaten to do it.

Proverbs 4:23 – Out of the heart are the issues of life. We commit sin because we allow ourselves to desire in our hearts to commit sin.

Matthew 12:35-37 – The mouth speaks out of the abundance of the heart. We will be justified or condemned by our words. We are wrong if we say we will do something wrong, even if we never actually do it.

Why do people threaten to seek divorce? Usually to hurt their partner. We can hurt others by words, not just by deeds. This is cruel and unloving.

In the absence of Scriptural grounds for divorce, Christians should never do or say anything that appears to justify separation or divorce. Instead, they should deliberately express and promote commitment. "I really do love you. I want to work out our problems, and I want us to have a good marriage."

(See also Matthew 5:21,22,27,28,33-37, etc.)

God Has a Pattern for Authority in the Home.

Ephesians 5:22-24 – The wife must submit to her husband as to the Lord.

1 Peter 3:1 – She must obey her husband even if he is not serving God. Sometimes a wife may think she may disobey her husband just because he commits sin, but God says she must still obey him. She may disobey only if the husband asks her to commit sin (Acts 5:29).

We will see that resolving conflict requires decisions to be made. God has provided a way to make those decisions. Sometimes husbands lack the ***courage*** or the strength of character to make tough decisions that need to be made. They allow their wives to dominate, even when they know sin exists that should end. And sometimes wives lack the strength of character and the humility to accept their husbands' decisions.

We will see that the husband also has God-given guidelines to follow when he makes decisions. Conflict may arise or remain unresolved either because the husband disobeys Bible teachings about how to make decisions or because the wife disobeys Bible teachings about submission.

(Titus 2:5; Colossians 3:18; etc.)

Growing a Godly Marriage

Express Appreciation and Praise for What Is Good.

Philippians 4:6,7 – Let your requests be made known to God with **thanksgiving**. Even when we are concerned about our problems, we must remember to be thankful for our blessings.

Often in times of strife, we get so upset with our companion, that we fail to express appreciation for the good qualities they have. This tends to blow the problems out of proportion.

Husbands Should Express Appreciation for Their Wives.

Genesis 2:18 – It was not **good** for man to be alone, so God made woman to be a companion for him. God deliberately created woman to be **good** for her husband.

Proverbs 18:22 – He who finds a wife, finds a good thing and obtains favor of God. So let the husband **say** so.

Proverbs 12:4 – A worthy woman is the **crown** of her husband. If so, then let the husband express appreciation for her. (Proverbs 19:14; 31:10)

1 Peter 3:7 – The husband should give **honor** to his wife. Yet, one major failing many husbands have is that we give much more criticism than we give honor. This is absolutely one area in which I failed in the early years of our marriage.

Husbands, how often do you deliberately say or do something intended to **honor** your wife? Is she supposed to feel honored simply because you haven't **insulted** her recently?

Proverbs 31:28-31 – The husband of a worthy woman ought to give her **praise**. Do you **praise** your wife when she prepares a meal, cleans the house, cares for your children, or fulfills her responsibilities as a Christian? Or do you just criticize when you think she fails?

A husband usually gets a sense of fulfillment and accomplishment from his work. He gets a regular paycheck and perhaps occasional promotions. But the wife works day in and day out at home with the family. If the husband does not express appreciation, the wife should still find a sense of accomplishment in seeing her children develop and in knowing above all that God is pleased. But she has a much greater sense of security and accomplishment if her husband **tells** her he appreciates what she does.

Men, God instructs us to praise our wives when they do good. If we did, they would find it much easier to fulfill their role as submissive homemakers.

Wives Should Express Appreciation for Their Husbands.

Romans 13:7 – All Christians should give honor to whom honor is due. This is a general principle. It teaches husbands to honor their wives, but it also teaches wives to honor their husbands.

Ephesians 5:33 – Because the husband is the head of the wife (verses 22-24), she should respect (reverence) him. Surely this includes expressing appreciation for him.

Ladies, if your husband works regular hours at his job to provide for you and the family, how often do you tell him you appreciate it? Or do you just take his paycheck and spend it without a word of thanks? When he does repairs around the house, or spends time with the children, or fulfills his role as a Christian man, do you tell him you appreciate it?

Probably the greatest need that the wife has is a sense of **security** in knowing that she is loved and needed. Probably the greatest need the man has is the sense of being **respected** and looked up to. Both these needs are met if the husband and wife will express appreciation for one another.

If you are angry and upset with your companion, do two things. (1) Make an honest list of every good quality your companion possesses and every good work he/she does. Be as thorough as you can. (2) Then every day make a definite point to express love to your companion and find something specific to compliment and express appreciation for. This will significantly help when it comes time to discuss your problems, and it will also make your problems seem much less serious.

Act in Love.

Husbands should love their wives as Christ loved the church (Ephesians 5:25,28,29). Wives should also love their husbands (Titus 2:4). Love for one another is absolutely essential in solving serious conflict.

Love Is Concern for the Well-being of Others.

Ephesians 5:25,28,29 – Jesus' love for the church illustrates the love husbands should have for their wives. He loved us so much He gave His life so we could be saved. So, the husband should be concerned for the well-being of the wife. He should nourish and cherish her. He must use his authority, not just to please himself, but to do what is best for his wife and the family.

1 Corinthians 13:5 – Love is not selfish.

Romans 13:10 – Love works no harm to its neighbor.

As long as one or both companions selfishly insist on their own way, differences will not be resolved. Serious problems can be solved only when each is willing to seek the other's welfare, not just his/her own well-being.

Love Is a Choice of the Will.

Ephesians 5:25,28 – Love can be commanded because it is a matter of the *will*. We can choose whether or not to love, just like we choose whether or not to obey any other command.

Some think love just happens: you "fall in love" or out of love. This view makes us victims of circumstances: we are not in control. So, if a couple "just don't love one another anymore," nothing can be done except to get a divorce. But when we realize we can *choose* to love, then we realize we *can put love into* a marriage. And if we fail to put it in, we *sin*.

Furthermore, just as Christ initiated love toward the church when we were sinners not acting lovingly toward Him, so *it is the primary responsibility of the husband to initiate love.* The command is emphasized to the man. He is to love the wife first and put love into the relationship, as Christ first loved the church.

Romans 5:6-8 – Christ loved us while we were yet sinners, not because we were so lovable that He couldn't help Himself. He *chose* to do what we needed done.

Luke 6:27,28 – We are commanded to love our enemies. Loving one's enemy is about what it would take to put love into some marriages! How do you love an enemy? Not by falling uncontrollably into love, but by *choosing* to do what is best for them.

Each spouse should understand that the statement "I just don't love her/him any more" is a confession of sin! It must be repented of and corrected as an act of the will!

When serious disagreements build up in marriage and are not resolved, one or both companions are not choosing to show love.

Love Must Be Expressed in Words and in Deed.

Love should be expressed by what we say.

Ephesians 5:25 – Husbands should love as Christ loved the church. But Christ states His love for the church (Ephesians 5:2; John 3:16). So husbands and wives should express love for one another in words.

Do not wait for an overwhelming romantic "feeling" that wells up and can't help but be expressed. We are discussing love by choice of the will. If so, then we choose to express that love.

We can and should state, by the choice of our will: "I want you to know that I still love you, I am committed to this marriage and to your welfare." Since the husband is to initiate love as Christ did, he must make a deliberate, conscious effort to tell his wife regularly – preferably every day – that he loves her. And she should do the same to him, sincerely from the heart.

Love should be expressed by what we do.

1 John 5:2,3 – Love for others requires us to love God and keep His commands. Keeping God's commands is loving God.

1 John 3:18 – We must not love just in words, but in deed and in truth. This is a vital principle in every home. We ought to say loving things, but that alone is not enough. We must act in love. Whatever we do and say in the marriage must be directed by God's will, motivated by love.

(Luke 10:25-37; 6:27,28)

Growing a Godly Marriage

Love Requires Giving and Self-sacrifice.

Giving of self is the essence of love.

Ephesians 5:25 – Jesus loved the church and **gave** Himself for it.

John 3:16 – God so loved the world that He **gave** His only-begotten Son.

1 John 3:14-18 – If you see your brother in need and don't **give** what is needed, you don't have love. Surely this applies in the home. If I see my spouse in need and don't give what he/she needs, I do not have love (notice that says "need," not "want").

Romans 12:20 – Even loving your enemy requires **giving** food and drink when needed.

Note that this requires giving our **time and effort** for the good of the other person. Many marriages face serious problems because husband and/or wife are too busy doing other things – maybe even useful things (like work, caring for children, etc.) – to develop and maintain a good relationship with one another.

Spouses must determine to take time for one another. This is a requirement of love, and love is a Divine command in a marriage. If you are too busy to spend some private time regularly with your spouse, you need to rearrange your schedule!

A basic requirement in solving family disagreements is a willingness to give of ourselves for the good of others.

Typically, each spouse refuses to change because he/she is upset at something the other person did. If we would view the situation honestly and objectively (as if it were someone else's problem), we might see that we are in the wrong. But we refuse to admit our error or to change because of some habit or characteristic we dislike in our spouse.

The fundamental lesson of Christ's love is that we should give up our own desires for the good of others even when they are not acting the way we think they should. Don't say, "I'll change if he/she will too." If an act would be helpful, **do it** regardless of what they do. If we have been wrong, **admit it** regardless of whether or not they ever admit their errors.

Even if we are convinced we are not the root cause of a problem, we should ask ourselves honestly what we can do to help improve it. This does not mean ignoring sin. Jesus did not cause our sin problem and He did not compromise with sin, but He did sacrifice Himself to provide a **solution** to our sin problem. He did not just sit back and criticize us for our sin, but He became involved to provide a solution. He did not do everything for us, but He made sure we had a way whereby we could overcome the problem.

A mistake I often made early in our marriage was to just criticize without offering help in solving the problem: "Here's the problem and I expect you to solve it." Even if that is true, is it helpful? Instead think, "What can I offer to do – how can I become involved – so as to help resolve this problem?" Instead of saying, "Why don't you do this?" say, "Why don't you and I work on this **together**?"

As long as neither spouse will take the first step to give up what they want, strife will continue. When one is willing to give in for the good of the group, then a start has been made toward resolving the problem. When both are willing to give in for the good of the group, then the solution definitely will be found.

The husband has the final say, but he must not just do what he wants. He must put aside his own desires and do what is best for the group. The wife must not insist on what she wants, but must give in and submit to the husband's decisions.

(1 John 4:9,19; Acts 20:35; Luke 10:25-37)

Growing a Godly Marriage

Discuss the Problem

Be Willing to Discuss.

Sometimes a spouse becomes so angry that he/she refuses to talk. Some men think they have the right to just make a decision without discussion.

The husband should be willing to consider his wife's views.

Ephesians 5:25ff – The husband is head as Jesus is head of the church. But God listens to our requests in prayer (Philippians 4:6,7).

Ephesians 5:28,29 – The husband should love his wife as he does his own body, but the body communicates its needs so the head can make decisions according to what is best.

James 1:19 – Every man should be swift to **hear**, slow to speak, slow to anger.

1 Peter 3:7 – The husband is to treat his wife with understanding. But since men are not mind readers, this requires listening to the wife's views.

When a man has the attitude that he does not need to discuss with his wife about decisions that affect her, he shows a general misunderstanding of Scripture. But when serious problems exist in the home, that approach can be even more dangerous. Serious problems can be resolved only when both spouses are willing to communicate about the problem.

(Compare Matthew 7:12.)

If sin is involved, both parties are commanded to discuss.

Luke 17:3,4 – The one who believes the other has sinned, must **rebuke** him. Why wouldn't that apply to sin in the home as well as elsewhere? (Leviticus 19:17,18; Matthew 18:15; Proverbs 27:5,6)

Matthew 5:23,24 – One who has been accused of sin must be willing to talk to seek reconciliation. Again, why would that not apply in the home?

Note that the person who believes he has been wronged and the person who is accused of doing wrong are both obligated to discuss the matter. If conflict in the home is to be resolved, it must begin by discussion. "Clamming up" is not an option.

Note, however, that proper **timing** of when to discuss is also important. Discussing in front of the kids or when one of you is extremely angry may not be good. If so, don't just "clam up" or stalk out of the room and refuse to discuss. Instead, agree to discuss the matter **later**, and **set a time** when you will discuss it. **Make an appointment and keep it!**

This does not mean that matters must be discussed endlessly. As we will consider later, steps must be found whereby the issue will be resolved. But both must be willing to discuss in order to determine what caused the problem and to find a solution.

(Matthew 18:15-17; Proverbs 10:17; Galatians 6:1; Proverbs 13:18; 15:31,32; 29:1; 25:12; 9:8; 12:1)

Speak to Resolve the Problem, Not to Hurt One Another.

Matthew 5:24 – The goal is to be **reconciled**, not to hurt people. Often we are willing to talk, but only for the purpose of **getting our way** or raking our spouse over the coals. We seek to win a victory, prove the other person wrong, etc. The purpose ought to be to find a Scriptural resolution. (Leviticus 19:18)

Romans 12:17,19-21 – Don't repay evil for evil or seek vengeance, but return good for evil. Sometimes a couple starts out trying to resolve a problem, but one insults the other, then the other returns an insult. Soon the goal becomes to see who can hurt the other person worst.

Too many discussions end up being quarrels, because we let the problem become an occasion to **attack one another**. Instead, we should work together to **attack the problem**. Discuss the problem to solve the problem, not to hurt one another's feelings.

When bringing up a problem, introduce it objectively then maintain focus on the specific problem. "Honey, there's a problem we need to talk about..." Don't enlarge the problem to attack the character of the other person. Avoid "You're just selfish, that's all," or "Why can't you be like so-and-so's wife?" or "You're just like your mother!" or "Why do you always have to ...?"

Listen to Your Spouse's Viewpoint.

A "discussion" requires both listening and talking. In practice, however, many spouses only want to express **their own** views.

Growing a Godly Marriage

James 1:19 – Let every man be swift to hear, slow to speak, slow to wrath. Don't enter the discussion assuming the other person has no valid reasons for his view. We should be quickly willing to listen, and slow to present our views, especially when we are angry.

Suggestion: **Begin the discussion by asking your spouse to explain his/her view**. Do not begin by attacking the position you assume they hold and defending your own view. Begin by asking questions honestly designed to help you understand what they think. "Could you explain to me why you did it that way?" "Have you considered doing it like this?" Maybe they have considered your idea and have some valid reasons for preferring another approach.

Do not dominate the discussion. Let the other person express his/her views. Do you appreciate it when others just attack your views but refuse to listen to what you have to say? "Love your neighbor as yourself," and practice the golden rule (Matthew 7:12).

Honestly Discuss the Evidence.

John 7:24 – "Do not judge according to appearance, but judge with righteous judgment."

Honestly seek to learn the facts of what happened.

Maybe the other person did not do what you thought they did. Ask for the reasons why the other person holds his/her view. Maybe they have reasons that you have not considered.

Then present **evidence** for your view. Don't just make charges and accusations. Don't jump to conclusions or assign motives. **If you don't have proof, then ask questions.** But don't make accusations unless you have proof. Recognize an obligation to prove what you say or else don't say it!

Matthew 18:16 – By the mouth of two or three witnesses every word may be established (Acts 24:13). Do not consider your spouse guilty of wrongdoing until the evidence is clear. Do not condemn them on the basis of opinion and flimsy appearances, when you would not want them to condemn you on that basis.

2 Timothy 3:16,17 – The Scriptures must guide us in matters of right and wrong. They will judge us in the last day (John 12:48). If there are Bible principles relating to the subject, study them together.

Volume does not constitute proof.

Sometimes one or both spouses will try to get his/her way by talking loudly, talking long, bringing a matter up over and over and over, or repeatedly interrupting the other. The result amounts to intimidation, browbeating, bullying, or nagging. We attempt to win by wearing the other person down, frightening them, or making them miserable, so we hope they give in.

Matthew 6:7 – Some people "think they will be heard for their many words." God does not answer prayer for such people, so why should we just accept what they say?

Proverbs 21:9 – It is better to dwell in a corner of a housetop than in a house shared with a contentious woman.

Proverbs 19:13 – The contentions of a woman are a continual dripping. A form of Chinese torture was to have drops of water repeatedly drip on a man's forehead. That is how Scripture describes nagging.

Proverbs 10:19 – In the multitude of words sin is not lacking, but he who restrains his lips is wise.

Just because you can talk longer and louder than others does not prove you are right! Both spouses must be willing to listen and to speak honestly to resolve the problem.

(Proverbs 20:3; 21:19; 17:27)

Honestly Examine Your Own Conduct, Motives, Etc.

Consider honestly the possibility that you may have been wrong, or that you may at least have contributed to the problem. Do not just find fault with your mate. Perhaps you can improve.

Genesis 3:12,13 – When the first married couple sinned, God confronted them. The man blamed the woman and the woman blamed the serpent. **Both had been wrong, but neither was willing to admit their wrong**. That is typical. Even when we are guilty, we want others to bear or share the blame – "Look what he/she did!"

Proverbs 28:13 – He who covers his sins will not prosper, but whoever confesses and forsakes them will have mercy. When a family has serious problems, almost invariably there is sin, but the guilty one(s) refuses to admit it, blames others, rationalizes, etc. (2 Corinthians 13:5)

Pride keeps us from recognizing and admitting our guilt. Most people, when studying a topic like this one, can think of lots of points that apply to their spouses, but what about **you**? (Interesting how many people, after hearing a lesson on subjects like this, will respond that their spouse really needed to hear that lesson! It may have been said in humor, but are we examining ourselves?)

Honesty and humility lead us to seek the truth and admit whatever errors we have made. And remember, even if we are not convinced we caused a problem, love leads us to be willing to get involved and help solve it.

(1 Thessalonians 5:21; Psalm 32:3,5; Galatians 6:1)

Be Patient and Control Your Temper.

1 Corinthians 13:4 – Love is patient. Often we become easily upset when a matter is not quickly resolved. Resolving some problems may take a long time, with gradual improvement. Don't give up. Don't

expect that you or your spouse will change overnight. Give it time. (Romans 2:7; Galatians 6:7-9; 2 Thessalonians 3:5)

Proverbs 18:13 – To answer a matter before we have heard it is foolish. Sometimes we are ready to judge a matter before we have thought it through. Don't make snap decisions.

Don't think that you must reach a final decision the first time a matter is brought up. Take time for both you and your spouse to think through what has been discussed. If your initial discussion doesn't lead to a solution, ask for time to think about it. Make a commitment to discuss it again later. You are more likely to reach a rational conclusion, and your spouse will know you have taken the matter seriously.

Proverbs 15:1 – A soft answer turns away wrath, but a harsh word stirs up anger. Don't allow your temper to make you lose your objectivity and resort to hurting the other person. Anger is not necessarily sinful, but it must be controlled so it doesn't lead us into sin (Ephesians 4:26; James 1:19,20).

Be Reconciled

The goal is, not just to talk endlessly nor simply to vent frustrations, but to **resolve** the problem. You should seek to determine a **plan of action** whereby the problem ceases to alienate you. This involves several principles.

Compromise or Overlook Differences of Viewpoint, Where Possible.

Scriptures

1 Corinthians 13:4,5 – Love suffers long and is kind. Love is not selfish.

Ephesians 4:2,3 – We should be longsuffering and bear with one another. Every couple will find in one another characteristics that we would like to change; but either they cannot be changed, or it is not worth the trouble it would cause to try to change them. Sin must not be overlooked, but if there is no sin and the person does things we just don't **like**, then love will not push personal desires to the point of alienation. Learn to overlook these matters without bitterness.

Proverbs 29:11 – A fool vents all his feelings, but a wise man holds them back. Some people brag about how "I say just what I think." It never occurs to them that some things are better left unsaid. Other people speak without thinking of the consequences. Some opinions and some characteristics and some differences are just not important enough to cause conflict about.

Romans 14 – Even some spiritual decisions are matters of personal judgment, not matters of sin. If you cannot prove your spouse has committed sin, do not imply he/she has been guilty.

James 3:17 – Wisdom from above is first pure, then **peaceable and willing to yield**. Christians want peace with those around them, especially in their own families. Purity must come first – we do not overlook sin. But when a matter is not sinful, seek a peaceable resolution. We should want the conflict to end, even if we have to give up our own desires to achieve it.

(Matthew 5:9; Romans 12:17-21; 1 Peter 3:11)

Applications

"***Choose your battles.***" Don't just complain over everything your spouse does that irritates you. Decide how serious an issue really is. Is it worth the conflict and disagreement that may result? If not, just drop it. But if you choose this course, then do not be bitter or resentful.

Be willing to compromise – give and take – as long as no Bible conviction is violated. Seek a middle-ground solution. "I'll give in here, if you'll give in there." Or, "Let's do it your way this time, and then next time we'll do it my way." Some people do this in matters of Biblical right or wrong; however, we will see that we must **not** compromise regarding sin. But simple differences of view are another matter.

Our family used to have a lot of conflict over what movie to watch on family nights or what restaurant to eat at on trips. We found the solution: take turns. This time it is one person's turn, next time another person's turn, etc. There is no arguing. Each person knows he/she will get his turn but will also have to agree without fussing when it is someone else's turn. "Well, we would just argue about whose turn it is!" Then write it down – keep a record.

Perhaps, in some matter, you will end up each going separate ways and doing separate things.

Remember to consider ways you can become involved and help your spouse do a job better. Instead of just sitting back and criticizing, discuss what you can do to help your spouse deal with a problem (Acts 15:36-40).

However, if one has been guilty of sin, then another approach must be taken.

Repent of Sin.

Start by examining yourself.

Instead of blaming your spouse for every problem, consider your own conduct before you criticize his or hers.

2 Corinthians 13:5 – Examine yourselves as to whether you are in the faith. Prove yourselves. If a problem involves accusation of sin, we are obligated before God to consider our own guilt. Remember, guilt is determined by Scripture, not by our opinions or those or our spouse.

Matthew 7:3-5 – Do not just consider the speck in another person's eye, but first remove the plank from your own eye. Otherwise, you are a hypocrite, criticizing others for error, when you are just as guilty or worse.

Most of us are experts at minimizing our error while maximizing the "errors" of others. "Well, maybe I did make a mistake, *but* look what *you* did!" My errors are "mistakes," but yours are big, black *sins!*

Most of us know we should not think this way regarding relationships outside the home, but why shouldn't the same be true at home? If I am wrong to criticize others when I too am guilty, then should I not correct my faults at home as well as in other relationships?

Recognize your errors and humbly determine to change.

Acts 8:22 – If one or both have sinned, the Bible says to repent and pray for forgiveness. Why should sins in the family be any different?

2 Corinthians 7:10 – Godly sorrow works repentance unto salvation. Repentance is a decision and commitment to *change*. We must recognize we have been wrong and agree to do right. If sin is the cause of our problems, we will never correct our marriage until we repent.

One lesson I learned the hard way (though maybe not yet as well as I need to learn it) is that the first step to solving a difference with someone else is to recognize and admit where I have been wrong. I need to "clean my slate" first, then I can help the other person with any corrections they need to make.

(Luke 13:3; Acts 17:30; 2 Peter 3:9)

Apologize for Sin (Confess It).

Luke 17:3,4 – If we have sinned, we must say, "I repent." Sometimes we realize we were wrong, but we are too proud to admit it. Until we do so, those whom we have wronged cannot know we have repented. But that's not all.

Matthew 5:23,24 – When we have wronged someone, we must go to them and make it right, or God will not accept our worship. Note it: God does not accept my worship if I refuse to correct the wrongs I have done to others. We know this applies in other relationships; why not in the home? Have you made right the wrongs you have done to your family?

James 5:16 – We must confess our sins one to another. Sometimes the most difficult people to apologize to are the ones closest to us. We think if we admit error, they will lose respect for us. This is simply *pride*. But love is not puffed up (1 Corinthians 13:4).

Or we think they are as much or more to blame than we are, so we expect them to admit their error first, then maybe we will admit ours. But God commands you to admit and confess your sin, whether or not your spouse ever admits sin. If you are guilty of sin and don't confess it, you stand condemned before God! Is it really worth it to persist in your stubborn pride when the result is that you stand guilty before your Creator and will give account in the day of judgment?

Proverbs 28:13 – He who covers his sins will not prosper, but whoever confesses and forsakes them will have mercy.

So, don't say, "I'll apologize if he/she will." I have seen cases where people in obvious sin would grudgingly admit error so long as everybody else – or at least somebody else – would apologize too. They think they can save face, because other people had to admit error. If I repent only on condition that other people repent, is that real repentance?

My confession must come from repentance and my repentance must come from godly sorrow. If I am truly sorry, then I must repent and confess whether or not anyone else does so. If I sinned, God commands me to say, "I repent" – no conditions on what others do. No "I'll repent *if* he repents." If I don't repent and confess, I remain in sin. If I say I will leave my sin only if other people will leave their sin, is that real repentance? If I really am sorry and repent, I won't be the last to apologize, and people won't have to bargain with me. I will willingly be the first to apologize!

Confessions should be specific. Don't minimize, make excuses, blame shift, or recriminate. Even if you are convinced your spouse is wrong too, honestly admit your own error and correct it. Don't try to save face. Don't **demand** that other people forgive you. Don't instruct them on how they ought to treat you. Just humbly apologize. Then later, perhaps at some other time, discuss the errors you believe they need to correct.

Pray for Forgiveness.

Acts 8:22 – Peter told Simon to repent and pray for forgiveness. If we have sinned, we must confess, not just to our spouse, but also to God.

1 John 1:9 – He is faithful to forgive us if we **confess** our sins.

Some of us let our pride keep us from admitting our sins, not only to our spouse, but also to God! God says to confess our sins or we remain in sin! When you have sinned, do you humbly confess it to God and to your spouse? (Matthew 6:12; Psalm 32:5)

Forgive One Another.

Time and again I have seen couples that have fought so long that one of them decides he or she will not forgive again, no matter what the spouse does or says. They may grieve for years about some error their spouse committed. Finally, the spouse humbly apologizes and asks forgiveness and they say, "I have put up with this so long, I just can't forgive him/her."

Luke 17:3,4 – When one has sinned against us and confesses, we must forgive, even seven times a day if necessary. Love forgives as often as is needed.

Matthew 18:21-35 adds that we must forgive 70 times 7 – i.e., without limit.

Colossians 3:13 – We must forgive the way God forgives. How do we want God to forgive us? Do we want Him to say, "I've forgiven you enough already. I don't care how sorry you are or how hard you try, I won't forgive"? Do we want Him to say He forgives, but then keep bringing it up again and using it as a weapon against us?

Matthew 6:12,14,15 – If we refuse to forgive others, God will simply not forgive us. Does this apply just outside the family? Why don't these principles apply in the family as well as in other relationships?

Illustration: When Indian tribes made peace, they would symbolize it by burying a hatchet (tomahawk). The point was that everybody knew where it was, but nobody would go dig it up and use it to hurt the others. So forgiveness does not mean we are no longer aware the thing happened. It means we will not bring it up again to hurt the other person with it.

Proverbs 10:12 – Hatred stirs up strife, but love covers all sins.

How is your family? Do you love one another enough to admit your errors and then to really forgive like you want God to forgive you? (Matthew 5:7)

Seek Help (If Necessary)

The procedure we have described will resolve most serious family problems, if we really love one another and are willing to obey God. But what if there clearly is **sin** in a family and the above procedure has been tried, but the problem remains? The Bible tells us to get help from other Christians.

Talk to one or two faithful Christians.

Galatians 6:2 – Bear one another's burdens. Our first source of help should be other Christians. Some are too embarrassed to have others find out about their problems, but one of the first steps to overcoming a problem is to admit we have it.

James 5:16 – Confess your faults to one another and pray for one another. Sometimes other Christians have had experience dealing with a problem and can give the Scripture or application that we need. Surely they can pray for us.

Sometimes, if they seek help at all, Christians will go to a counselor or psychiatrist who is not even a true Christian. Why should Christians with spiritual problems – especially sin problems – seek help first from counselors who do not truly follow Scripture? Many counselors complicate problems instead of solving them. In any case, if the problem is sin, who can help solve it better than other Christians?

Growing a Godly Marriage

Follow Matthew 18:15-17.

If your brother sins against you, first discuss it privately with him. But if this does not resolve it, ***get help***. Take one or two other Christians with you.

Many think this passage does not apply to family problems, but why not? It discusses cases where one Christian sins against another. Where does this, or similar passages, exclude family members from the application? Most of the Scriptures we have cited in this study have been general in application, not specifically regarding the family, yet we can all see they would apply to the family. Why is that not the case with this verse? (Compare 1 Corinthians 6:1-11)

We would hope that the help of one or two other Christians would solve the problem; but if it does not, then the Bible says to take the matter before the congregation. Perhaps the involvement of the whole church will bring the guilty party to his senses.

If even this does not solve the problem, then the one who is clearly in sin must be withdrawn from. (2 Thessalonians 3:15; 1 Corinthians 5; etc.)

This is not to say we should run to the church with every personal problem. Nor should we be quick to pursue such a course. We should be patient and give abundant opportunity for correction before such measures. But if ***sin*** is clearly involved and private efforts do not lead to repentance, God gives a pattern for proceeding. In far too many cases, sin continues in our families and we continue to suffer, because we are too proud or too foolish to pursue the Scriptural course for seeking help.

Develop and Carry Out a Plan to Correct the Problem.

Many marriage problems are deep-rooted, have continued for a long time, or have caused serious harm. Some spouses confess the same old sin over and over, then they go back and commit the same sin again and again. They never make specific provision to ***change.*** They seem to think that all they need to do is to admit the wrong from time to time and people should overlook it without requiring specific commitment regarding how the person intends to ***change.***

Proverbs 28:13 – He who covers his sins will not prosper, but whoever confesses and ***forsakes*** them will have mercy. No matter how often we confess a problem, it is not truly resolved until we change our conduct!

Matthew 21:28-31 – Jesus described a son who did not do what his father said. When he repented, he had to ***do*** what he failed to do. When we repent of wrongs, we must work to make sure they are not repeated. For long-standing habits, change will require planning and effort. (Compare Ephesians 4:25-32; Matthew 12:43-45)

Acts 26:20 – One who repents must bring forth *"**fruits of repentance**"* or do "works worthy of repentance" (Luke 3:8-14; Matthew 3:8). This includes making sure that we do not repeat the wrong in the future. But it also includes doing what we can to overcome the harm caused by our wrong deeds of the past. (Compare Ezekiel 33:14,15; 1 Samuel 12:3; Philemon. 10-14,18,19; Luke 19:8.)

When a couple has long-standing and deep-seated problems, resolution must include a mutual agreement about what they specifically intend to do differently in the future to change the conduct. They need *a specific program or plan of action*, perhaps even one that is written down.

Alternative courses of action should be discussed. Ways each spouse can help the other should be agreed upon. Agreements should include exactly what each partner will do differently in the future. Preferably, these should be stated in a way that allows for progress to be obvious or measurable – it should be evident when the changes are (or are not) being carried out. Then the couple should made specific **commitments or promises** to one another to carry out these actions.

James 5:12 – But let your "Yes," be "Yes," and your "No," "No." When we make commitments to one another, we must mean what we say and then must carry out our commitments. We must make the changes we promised to make and fulfill the plan of action we agreed upon. (Romans 1:31,32; 2 Corinthians 8:11)

Conclusion

Our homes were intended by God to be a great blessing to us, and specifically to help us serve Him faithfully and receive eternal life. But I am convinced that many people – including people that know how to treat other people in other relationships – will be lost right in their own homes, because of how they treat their spouses and children.

But the Scriptures provide us to all good works, including how to solve problems in our homes. There is no need for couples, both of whom profess to be Christians, to live year after year with serious alienation between them. Even less is there excuse for divorce, simply because couples have "irreconcilable differences." The result simply causes increased pain and grief to the couple, to their children, to the church, and to all who know them.

There is hope for troubled marriages. We can solve our problems God's way. If we do not do so, we have no one to blame but ourselves.

What about your home and your marriage? Do you need to make changes? Do you need to begin by receiving forgiveness of your sins and becoming a child of God? If you have done that, are you living faithfully in your home and in all your relationships?

Growing a Godly Marriage

Leave and Cleave

Introduction:

Genesis 2:24 instructs a man to leave his father and mother and cleave (be joined) to his wife. Jesus repeated this instruction in Matthew 19:5 and Paul repeated it in Ephesians 5:31.

I increasingly see evidence that people need to make better applications of this passage.

Consider with me some lessons people need to learn about what it means to leave father and mother and cleave to one's wife.

An Overview of God's Will for Marriage

Marriage Is Ordained of God and Must Follow His Will.

Genesis 2:18-24; 1:16-28 – God created marriage from the beginning. Since He created it, He knows the best way to conduct it.

2 Timothy 3:16,17 – The Scriptures are profitable to instruct us and provide us completely to all good works. That includes marriage.

Psalm 127:1 – Except the Lord builds the house, they labor in vain that build it.

Many people seek to follow Bible teaching regarding salvation, the church, worship, etc. But do we likewise follow God's plan for our homes?

Marriage Is a Lifetime Bond Between One Man and One Woman.

Genesis 2:24 – From the beginning, God intended marriage to consist of one man and one woman who *cleave* ("joined" – NKJV; "hold fast" – ESV) to one another and become one flesh.

Romans 7:2,3 – Marriage is for life. A person who is bound to a spouse in marriage must never seek another companion while their first companion lives. (Other passages list fornication as an exception, but we should never wish for that.)

Hebrews 13:4 – The sexual union is permissible only in the lifetime marriage of one man to one woman. Any other arrangement constitutes fornication or adultery which God will judge.

(Matthew 19:3-9; 5:31,32; Mark 10:2-12; Luke 16:18; 1 Corinthians 7:3-5,10,11; Malachi 2:14-16)

The Man Should Work to Provide for Himself and His Family.

Genesis 3:17-19 – From the beginning the man was responsible to labor with his hands to provide bread. A man who is able to do this but will not, is lazy and foolish (Proverbs 24:30-34).

Ephesians 5:28-31 – The man should also "nourish and cherish" his wife as he does himself. These terms include providing and caring for her, as well as protecting her.

1 Timothy 5:8 – The man who will not provide for his own, especially his own household, is worse than an unbeliever.

The Bible is filled with examples of men who were employed in various occupations by which they provided for their families: sailors, shepherds, physicians, tax collectors, carpenters, fishermen, preachers, etc.

(1 Thessalonians 4:10-12; 2 Thessalonians 3:10)

The Man Is the Head of His Family, and Parents Have Authority Over Children.

The husband is the head over his wife.

Genesis 3:16 – God decreed that the man should rule over his wife.

Ephesians 5:22-25,28,29 – The wife should submit to her husband as the church should submit to Christ. She must submit in "everything" unless her husband tells her to do something sinful (Acts 5:29). But the husband must rule with love like Jesus leads the church.

1 Peter 3:1-7 – Even if her husband disobeys God, the wife still must submit. But the husband should lead with honor for his wife and understanding for her needs.

(Colossians 3:18; Titus 2:5; 1 Corinthians 11:3,8-12.)

Growing a Godly Marriage

The parents exercise authority over their children.

Proverbs 1:8 – Children should hear the instruction of their fathers and not forsake the law of their mothers.

Ephesians 6:1,4 – Children are commanded to obey their parents. Fathers should bring their children up in the nurture and admonition of the Lord (Colossians 3:20).

Luke 2:51 – Jesus set an example of subjection to his parents.

(Genesis 18:19; Romans 1:30,32; Proverbs 22:6; Deuteronomy 4:9,10; 6:6-9; Psalm 78:4-8)

Each Family Should Function Independently from Other Families.

We emphasize that each of these Bible principles applies equally to each family.

* Each man is joined to **his** wife, and each woman is bound to **her** husband (Genesis 2:24; Romans 7:2,3). They are not bound or joined in marriage to any other man or woman.

* Each man must provide for **his** family (Ephesians 5:28-31; 1 Timothy 5:8). He does not have the same responsibility to provide for others.

* Each man should be the head of **his** wife, and each woman should submit to **her** husband (Genesis 3:16; Ephesians 5:22-25,28,29; 1 Peter 3:1-7; Titus 2:5). The man has no authority as head of any other woman, and the woman should submit as wife to no other man.

* Each father and mother are responsible to raise and train **their** children, and each child is responsible to obey **his** mother and father (Proverbs 1:8; Ephesians 6:1,4; Luke 2:51; Genesis 18:19). They have no authority as parents over the children of other families.

The result is that each family functions separately and independently from every other family.

Applications of the Principle of Leaving and Cleaving

Since these Bible principles apply to every family, Genesis 2:24 says that, when a man marries a woman, they form a new family separate from their parents' families. Each spouse must leave the family of his or her parents to establish a new family to which all these Bible principles apply separately and independently from their parents' families.

Consider the applications of these principles of marriage as they apply to this new family.

Permanence of Marriage

Matthew 19:3-9 – Jesus quoted Genesis 2:24 to prove that God forbids divorce. A man leaves his father and mother to be joined to his wife, and what God has joined together, man must not put asunder. The only exception is that one may divorce a companion for the cause of fornication. If one divorces for any other reason, the divorce is a sin. And when he remarries he commits adultery. And whoever marries the one whom he put away commits adultery.

Many young couples just live together without marriage. This is a failure to leave and cleave. The sexual union is permissible only within the lifetime marriage commitment of one man and one woman.

And often when young married couples have difficulties, as couples almost always do, one or the other runs home to live with his or her parents. The parents may even encourage this.

Divorce for any cause other than fornication is a failure to leave and cleave. And separation, except by temporary mutual agreement for spiritual purposes, is also a failure to leave and cleave because it fails to fulfill the spouse's needs and it tempts to fornication. (1 Corinthians 7:2-5)

Parents used to tell their children, "When you get married, if you have problems, don't come running home to mom and dad. Work your problems out."

The new husband and wife must leave their parents and cleave to their spouse.

Financial Independence

Parents should provide for their children while they are dependents subject to the parents' authority. But the time comes when a man is required by God to provide for himself.

2 Thessalonians 3:10 – If anyone will not work, neither shall he eat. Many able-bodied men continue living at home, supported by their parents, when they should be out looking for work to provide for themselves. Or they refuse to work because the available jobs are not to their liking.

1 Timothy 5:8 – In particular, when a man chooses to marry, he is commanded to provide for his wife and children. Yet often young couples get married knowing the husband is not able to provide for a family. And often they continue to depend on their parents to provide for them.

The man who marries must accept the responsibility to provide for his wife and children separately from his parents. There may be unexpected problems in any family, but to deliberately choose to continue to depend on the parents is a failure to leave and cleave.

Independent Authority

Independent authority goes hand in hand with financial independence.

Sometimes when young people are living at home and being supported by their parents, they decide that they have reached a certain age so they get to make their own rules and do not have to obey their parents. It does not work that way.

Just as the church has only one head, so each home has only one head – Ephesians 5:22-25. Everyone in the household must submit to the husband, just like everyone in the church must submit to Jesus. So, as long as you are living in your parents' home and depending on them to provide for you, you must follow their rules.

Fathers used to say, "As long as you put your feet under my table, you follow my rules."

That is one reason why it is a problem when a young man marries but he and his wife still live in the home of his or her parents. How can he be the head of his family when he himself is subject to his parents? This is a failure to leave and cleave.

Sometimes the new husband or new wife depends too much on their parents.

When a man marries, he becomes the head of his wife and children. Yet far too often the husband or the wife continues to depend on their parents for decisions.

Genesis 2:24 – When a man and woman marry, they form a new family separate from the families of either of their parents.

Ephesians 5:22-25 – This new family has a head and only one head: the husband. Neither the man's parents nor the wife's parents are the head of this new family. To submit to the parents would make two heads in one family. This is as wrong as if the church were to have two heads.

Sometimes a husband or wife has trouble "cutting the apron strings." The husband may make choices based on what pleases his parents instead of what pleases his wife and best meets the needs of his family. Or the wife may seek to please her parents, instead of her husband. This is a failure to leave and cleave.

Friends and family may make suggestions or give Biblical instruction when needed. But the husband is the head of the new family, and his decisions should primarily consider the needs and wishes of his wife and children.

Sometimes parents interfere with grown children's decisions.

Parents often struggle with allowing grown children to become independent.

For many years parents have exercised authority over their children. Often it is hard for them to let grown children go without continuing to interfere. They are unwilling to give up control. If the children have different family rules, the parents may instinctively think the children are unwise and even are reflecting negatively on the parents.

This is a difficult transition, but to continue to attempt to control their married children violates the principle of "leave and cleave."

Conflict can occur in many areas, but some areas can be especially troublesome:

Raising children

If the new family has different rules for their children, the grandparents may interfere. They may contradict their children's methods. Or they may deliberately try to influence the grandchildren to think or act differently from what their parents have taught them.

Sometimes grandparents want more time with their grandchildren and may resent restrictions that hinder their contact.

Ephesians 6:1,4 – God commands children to obey their parents, not their grandparents. Surely the grandparents may have wisdom to offer. But if they really are wise, they must remember that they no longer have the right to speak authoritatively. They may seek to advise or persuade calmly and patiently. But they must remember that their children are now in charge.

Religious differences

Parents sometimes view religion as a matter of family pride or family tradition. If grown children make different choices, the parents may feel rejected or failures as parents.

If parents believe their children's choices are sinful or spiritually dangerous, they should speak up; but they must do so respectfully, as they would address people in any other family. They have no right to use the fact they are parents as reason to demand submission.

Parents may think children dishonor them by choosing different courses.

Ephesians 6:2 – "Honor your father and mother." Some parents claim that grown children dishonor them or are disrespectful if they make decisions that the parents disapprove.

However, "honor" means to value, regard, or praise: the idea is appreciation or reward. Obedience and authority are not inherently part of the meaning. The word is often used for people who have no authority. Honoring someone does not mean we must obey or submit to them.

1 Timothy 5:3 – Honor widows who are really widows. This especially carries the idea of providing for their needs. Must we obey the widows?

1 Peter 2:17 – Honor all people. Does this mean we must obey all people?

John 12:26 – God honors those who serve Him. Does this mean God should obey us?

Matthew 15:3-6 – Jesus showed that honoring parents requires caring for them in old age, and He contrasted honoring parents to cursing them.

So honoring parents means appreciating or praising them and caring for them when needed. But it does not require children who have left their parents' household and are supporting themselves to obey their parents' instructions. To say otherwise would violate the principle of leaving and cleaving.

"Honor" (τιμαω) – "1 to set a price on, *estimate, value* ... 2 to show high regard for, *honor, revere ...*" – Bauer-Danker-Arndt-Gingrich

How should parents and grown children respond when they disagree?

Instead of calmly reasoning about disagreements, parents of grown children may try to get their way by manipulation and pressure. They may nag, bully, ridicule, make accusations, try to make children feel guilty, or even accuse them of sin. Unconsciously or not, this is an attempt to **control** their grown children.

Consider these Biblical principles:

1) Remember that parents and grown children make independent choices.

The children's family is a separate family from the parents as surely as any other family. To pressure or manipulate them would violate Biblical principles of leaving and cleaving.

1 Peter 4:15 – But let none of you suffer as a murderer, a thief, an evildoer, or as a busybody in other people's matters. Decisions of other families are their business. That includes our grown children. We must avoid pressuring them to accept our personal preferences.

2) Respect one another's personal conscience.

Romans 14:13,19 – Let us not judge one another anymore, but rather resolve this, not to put a stumbling block or a cause to fall in our brother's way. ... Therefore let us pursue the things which make for peace and the things by which one may edify another.

If your child chooses a course which is not sinful, it is just as wrong to ridicule or pressure them to violate their conscience as it is to disrespect the personal conscience of anyone else.

3) Follow all Biblical principles of reasoning based on God's word.

If you are convinced a child or parent is in sin or their choice is dangerous spiritually, then reason from Scripture like you should with any other Christian with whom you disagree.

James 1:19,20 – Let every man be swift to hear, slow to speak, slow to wrath.

Proverbs 10:19 – In the multitude of words sin is not lacking; he who restrains his lips is wise.

Acts 17:2,3 – Paul persuaded people by reasoning with them from the Scriptures.

2 Timothy 3:16,17 – The inspired Scriptures thoroughly equip us for every good work, including the good work of convincing and instructing people in righteousness.

Don't nag, yell, lose your temper, pressure, bully, or manipulate. Calmly reason from Scripture. Discuss like you would with any other Christian.

Conclusion

All of these concepts are important for parents to understand regarding their children. Young couples should also understand these principles. They may do well to discuss, even before marriage, how they will relate to their parents, families, and friends.

If a husband and wife have problems with in-laws, let them discuss these principles with those in-laws, explain the Bible teaching, and stand for what it teaches.

Let us learn to leave and cleave.

Growing a Godly Marriage

Seven Keys to Raising Godly Children

Introduction

Why this study is needed

Despite the fact that families in our society have material possessions unknown to previous generations, the fact is that many families face incredible conflict and hardship. These include:

* **Divorce** – Our society has reached the point that marriages are more likely to end by divorce than by death. (James Dobson letter, 11/99)

* **Crime** – In a recent 25-year period, the arrest rate among juveniles nearly tripled. (Bennett, p. 4)

* **Government dependence** – Recent statistics show that more than one child in eight was raised on government welfare. (Bennett, p. 5)

* **Births to unmarried women** – In a recent thirty-year period, the number of children born outside marriage increased by a factor of five. (Bennett, p. 9)

* **Single-parent families** – More than 1/3 of all children now do not live with their biological father. (Dobson letter)

* **Suicide** – In a recent 30-year period, the suicide rate among teens more than tripled. (Bennett, p. 12)

Many families do not have these problems, but the evidence shows that parent-child relationships are facing increasing hardships.

And Christians are by no means immune. In nearly every congregation, at least half the young people end up not serving God faithfully.

The subject of raising children deserves careful study.

Why you need to study this subject, regardless of who you are

* Are you a **parent**? Surely, you need to study about raising children.

* Are you a **young person**, not yet married? Someday almost surely you will be a parent or will work with children in some capacity (teacher, counselor, etc.). The time to prepare for an important task is *before* it begins. Why do young people go to school? They are being trained to prepare for future responsibilities in life. Likewise, the best time to begin preparing for parenthood is *before* you become a parent.

* Are you an **older person** with grown children or no children? You need to teach others God's will, including teaching about parental duties.

Titus 2:3-5 – Older women must be teachers of good things. Especially they must teach young women their duties as wives and mothers.

Acts 20:27 – All Christians should teach "the whole counsel of God." That includes Bible teaching about parenthood.

So if you have children or ever will have them – and even if you don't have them – as a Christian you need to know God's will about raising children. You need this study!

Our purpose is to learn how parents can raise children successfully despite the problems we face.

The foundational principle of these studies is that God's word provides the best way to raise children.

Proverbs 22:6 – Train up a child in the way he should go, and when he is old he will not depart from it. Despite the pressures that surround your family, by following God's word you can raise children who serve God faithfully.

Bible principles about child raising are so critical that we will refer to them as the "keys" to success. We will consider them under seven headings. So, "Seven Keys to Raising Godly Children."

Note: I do not claim perfection or expertise. I made many mistakes. Fortunately, my children have overcome most of them, and I hope they will be better parents than I was. Perhaps you can benefit from my mistakes. In any case, the standard to which we will appeal as our ultimate authority is God's word.

As in other areas, God's word includes general teachings and specific teachings.

God told Noah to "make" an ark of "gopher wood" (Genesis 6:14). Noah had to abide within the instructions God specified (such as "gopher wood"), but he had his choice of many tools or methods that would constitute "making" an ark.

Likewise, God teaches us to take the Lord's Supper on the first day of the week (Acts 20:7). That restricts us to the specified day, but by general authority we are free to decide what time on the first day of the week.

So also, when God states a principle regarding raising children, we must act within the teaching of that principle. Yet, in areas of general principles, different families may apply those principles differently and still be following God's word.

And in this study I may give advice that harmonizes with Bible principles, but that may not be the only way to apply them. But whatever we do must fit God's rules. If what we say or do disagrees with God's rules, then we are disagreeing, not with people, but with God.

So, let's consider together Seven Keys for Raising Godly Children.

(See the end of the study for sources cited and abbreviations used.)

Key #1: Purpose

No one can succeed in any task without focusing clearly on his goal.

Imagine a baseball team that becomes so wrapped up in their beautiful uniforms, beautiful ballpark, and making commercial endorsements that they neglect to win ballgames. Uniforms and a ballpark are helpful – even commercials may be all right – but the players must remember their goal is to win games!

So, parents must keep their goals clearly in mind. What do you consider to be your goal as a parent? When your life ends, how will you measure whether you have been a success or a failure as a parent?

Parents Must Set Goals.

Parents must have proper goals, and must work diligently toward those goals. Whether you like it or not, if you have children you are responsible to raise those children properly.

Too many parents simply don't want to accept their responsibility as parents. They expect others to raise their children: the government, schools, church, babysitters, day-care centers, or friends and relatives. Meanwhile the parents pursue other interests.

Some fathers leave the children to the mothers to raise (or vice versa). Some parents forsake their children by divorce or desertion. Some spend too much time away from home pursuing other interests. Some simply don't bother. How does God view such conduct?

You Brought These Children into the World.

When you participated in the act that produces children – even if you did not intend to conceive, nevertheless, if you chose to participate in the reproductive act – then you are responsible for any child that results. Your children did not ask to come here. You brought them here. Now it's your job to take care of them.

The government did not bring your child into this world. You did. So, don't expect the government to raise your child. Likewise, for the church, the schools, the day-care center, and your parents or relatives – none of them brought your children into this world. You brought them here; now you take care of them. Caring for them properly must be your goal.

God Holds You Responsible for Raising Your Children.

Titus 2:4 – Young women should be taught to love their children. Love requires caring for them, not deserting or neglecting them. This is something that can and must be learned. Women who do not learn it will cause God's word to be blasphemed (verse 5).

Ephesians 6:4 – Fathers are commanded to bring their children up in the nurture and admonition of the Lord. You cannot leave this up to others, including your wife (though, of course, she is responsible too). You are responsible. You have no right to shirk this duty or try to shift it to others.

Genesis 18:19 – God approved of Abraham, because he commanded his children to keep the way of the Lord. He did not leave this duty up to others.

1 Samuel 3:12-14 – On the other hand, when Eli's sons became corrupt, God held Eli accountable. God rebuked Eli, not the schools or the government or even just Eli's wife.

Parents, you must accept the goal of raising your children properly and must diligently work toward that goal. You must not leave this to others.

Some Goals Are Proper but Are Not the Main Goal.

Parents May Have Various Goals in Raising Children.

Some parents emphasize misguided or unimportant goals, such as physical beauty, athletic achievement, popularity, etc. But there are other goals that are really proper goals for parents to pursue for their children:

* We should meet our children's physical needs.

* We should provide a good education.

* We should prepare them for life, so they can have a happy marriage and be good citizens and neighbors.

* We may even provide some recreation, entertainment, and enjoyment.

1 Timothy 5:8 – If any does not provide for his own, and especially for his household, he has denied the faith and is worse than an unbeliever.

Christians should provide wholesome benefits for our children (Matthew 7:9-11).

But None of These Constitutes the Primary Goal of Parents.

Many parents are too concerned about physical pursuits.

Luke 12:15 – Jesus said, "Take heed and beware of covetousness, for one's life does not consist in the abundance of the things he possesses." He then told of a man who obtained great wealth but neglected God (verses 16-21). When the man died, what good did his wealth do him?

Matthew 16:26 – What is a man profited if he gains the whole world and loses his own soul? Likewise, what profit are we to our children if we give them all the world has to offer, but they are eternally lost?

Many parents work long hours to provide their children physical things, but they are so busy working that they neglect to give their children time and attention.

Other parents spend many hours with their children in physical pursuits: sports, clubs, school functions, music, etc. They are constantly on the run, but the emphasis is material, physical, and social.

I know one lady in the church whose daughter was named high school homecoming queen. The mother said this was the most wonderful thing that ever happened to her. When success in temporal things is our greatest joy, why should we expect our children to care about serving God! And sure enough, that woman's daughter never became a Christian.

The result of these approaches is exactly what we see in society: children who have hosts of physical advantages but are neither godly nor happy.

On the other hand, many "poor" families are highly successful.

I have known families with one old car, no TV, 4-room house, plain clothes, and just a basic education. But the children knew God's will, had close family ties, and grew up serving God faithfully.

Many children today are spoiled by over-providing. They don't appreciate what they are given and grow up thinking the world owes them a living.

Deuteronomy 18:10 – "There shall not be found among you anyone who makes his son or his daughter pass through the fire..." Most of us would not think of sacrificing a child to an idol. But covetousness is idolatry (Colossians 3:5). Too many parents over-emphasize material pursuits: possessions, toys, education, popularity, beauty, sports, etc. Unknowingly, such parents are sacrificing their children to the idols of covetousness and worldliness.

The Main Goal Is to Train Children to Serve God So They Can Receive Eternal Life.

Consider God's Goals for Parents.

Proverbs 22:6 – Train up a child in **the way he should go**, and when he is old he will not depart from it. You and I as parents will not always be around to guide our children's decisions. We must instill in them the understanding and habit of doing right, so they will serve God when they make their own decisions.

Ephesians 6:4 – Bring your children up in the training and admonition of the **Lord**.

Genesis 18:19 – Abraham commanded his children to **keep the way of the Lord,** to do righteousness and justice. This should be the goal of all fathers who are truly faithful to God.

Psalms 34:11 – Come, you children, listen to me; I will teach you **the fear of the Lord**. To accomplish this, we must give our children many things money cannot buy: time, love, instruction in God's word, guidance in dealing with life's problems, an example of godliness, and training in moral purity.

Joshua 24:15 – Joshua declared, "As for me and my house, we will **serve the Lord**." We should keep this goal constantly before us. With each decision we should ask, "What effect will this have on my child's eternal destiny?"

Malachi 2:15 – What does God seek when He joins a man and woman in marriage? He seeks **godly offspring**.

Our children were not given us to do with as we please. They are not our property. They are God's children given into our care, so we can raise them to be what **He** wants them to be.

Suppose our children grow up, get good jobs, have happy marriages, and are good neighbors and citizens, but do not live as faithful Christians. Then they are failures, and we have failed to accomplish our purpose as parents.

On the other hand, suppose our children don't receive college educations, live below middle-class American standards, and are not particularly athletic or outwardly beautiful, but they serve God faithfully. If so, they are successes, and we have been successful parents.

Throughout these studies our goal will be to emphasize principles that will help parents lead their children to put God first in life. We are studying how to raise *godly* children.

(Deuteronomy 4:10; 6:7ff; 11:18ff; Titus 1:6; Psalm 78:4ff; Jeremiah 32:39; 2 Timothy 3:15; Matthew 19:13ff)

Consider Then the Seriousness of This Responsibility.

Your choices as a parent may determine your children's eternal destiny.

Proverbs 23:13,14 – Do not withhold correction from a child. You shall beat him with a rod and deliver his soul from hell.

Proverbs 22:6 – Train up a child in the way he should go, and when he is old he will not depart from it.

Because so many children do not turn out well, people frequently emphasize that there are exceptions to this passage.

I believe that a diligent study of proverbs shows that many of them do have exceptions (20:28; 21:2; 22:7,11). To say there are no exceptions to Proverbs 22:6 would imply that the eternal destiny of children can be totally determined by parents, leaving the children without free will.

When children do not turn out well, we should all surely sympathize. The parents need to consider if they made mistakes. If they did, they should repent and ask forgiveness. What parents don't make mistakes?

But the fact remains that Proverbs 22:6 is a general statement of truth!

It is written to give parents confidence that, if they follow God's word, they can raise children to serve God and be saved! In our effort to console the parents of ungodly children, let us take care that we don't give the impression that raising godly children is nearly impossible.

I know a preacher who said repeatedly, "Every family has a black sheep." What passage teaches that? None! But he believed it, and sure enough he raised two "black sheep." If you think you cannot raise godly children, you are defeated before you start!

Growing a Godly Marriage

Regardless of occasional exceptions, the *rule* is that, if we do our job right, our children will be saved.

The fact so many people want to talk about the exceptions to the passage reveals much about the problems in the Lord's church. We are losing the majority of children, and there is no way the verse can justify that!

Instead of making excuses, let us just admit that many parents are not doing their job well. Let us learn from our mistakes and start studying God's word to find out how to do it right!

"Wouldn't it be terrible to have a child who was born with a serious physical or mental handicap or who died young?" Yes. But how infinitely worse to know my child faces torment in a Devil's hell! I cannot imagine any more terrible tragedy that could happen to one of my children. And I may very well determine whether or not that happens.

Your choices as a parent may determine your own eternal destiny!

1 Samuel 3:12-14 – Note that Eli himself was rejected for his children's sins, because he had failed as a parent! (Compare 2:22-25).

Ecclesiastes 12:14 – God will bring every work into judgment, and that includes our work as parents. When we stand before God to give account for our lives, He will judge us for our diligence as parents.

My job as a parent is to raise my children to serve God throughout this life and to be with Him in eternity. If I don't get my priorities straight so that I raise them to serve God first, He will hold **me** accountable.

To a large extent, your children's destiny **and your destiny** depend on whether or not you train your children as God's word says.

Conclusion

Let us not make the mistake of the baseball team that forgot its real purpose. Let us realize the seriousness of our responsibility as parents and keep our eye on our goal. If we have gotten off the track and put too much emphasis on temporal things, let us repent. And let us all accept the challenge to raise godly children.

Philippians 4:13 – I can do all things through Christ who strengthens me.

Key #2: Planning

When our children were small, L. A. Stauffer gave us this advice about raising children: "Just keep **thinking** and you'll be all right." This oversimplifies, but the point is that being a good parent requires thought and planning.

The Importance of a Good Plan

Every Important Work Needs to Be Planned.

To succeed in any important, difficult endeavor, we must first determine our **goal**. Then we must develop a **plan** for reaching our goal.

Planning is important in everyday life.

* If a business is to succeed, it must have a goal and a plan for reaching that goal.

* In building a house, one must have a blueprint to follow.

* Consider the years of planning needed to send a spaceship to the moon.

Often we fail to reach our goals because we fail to develop a clear plan for reaching them.

God planned His work:

Hebrews 8:5 – God had a plan for the tabernacle.

1 Peter 1:18-20 – God had a plan for our redemption before the world began. (Ephesians 1:7-9)

Ephesians 3:10,11 – The church was part of God's eternal purpose.

Romans 8:28 – God purposed to call us to salvation (through the gospel – 2 Thessalonians 2:13,14).

Our service to God requires planning.

Proverbs 14:22 – We receive mercy and truth if we devise (plan) good.

Luke 14:26-33 – We must count the cost of discipleship before we begin.

Psalms 17:3 – David purposed not to transgress with his mouth. This was no accident. He planned it that way.

2 Corinthians 9:7 – We should even plan the amount we give to the church.

Yet amazingly, hosts of parents, including members of the church, enter into marriage and parenthood with very little thought, study, or discussion about how they plan to succeed in raising their children. How much time and effort have you and your spouse spent in discussing exactly what rules and principles you will follow in raising your children?

(Acts 11:23; 1 Corinthians 14:33,40)

Satan has a plan for defeating our efforts to raise godly children.

Ephesians 6:12 – We do not wrestle against flesh and blood, but against principalities, against powers, against the rulers of the darkness of this age, against spiritual hosts of wickedness in the heavenly places.

In particular, Satan is battling us for the control of our children. When the children of Christians go astray, often the parents say, "I just don't understand what happened." Often what happens is that powerful forces are working against us that we either are not aware of or do not deal with effectively.

1 Timothy 6:12 – Fight the good fight of faith, lay hold on eternal life. Satan is determined to lead our children away from God. Parents must realize that we are in a *war* with Satan for the salvation of our children! To raise godly children, we must *fight evil*.

What army can win without a battle plan? We often lose our children because we don't recognize we are at war, so we have no plan for the fight!

2 Corinthians 2:11 – Satan will take advantage of us, if we are ignorant of his devices. Satan has devices – he has a plan! He knows exactly what methods work best to lead our children into sin. He has been using these methods successfully ever since Adam and Eve.

Do we really think we can defeat this wily, dangerous enemy without having a battle plan of our own? We must be aware of the means he uses to destroy our children's faithfulness, then we must have a plan for combating those influences.

Planning Is Required to Deal with Harmful Influences.

2 Corinthians 11:13-15 – Satan uses agents. He does not come directly and announce his evil intents. He uses devious, deceitful agents. Who are these agents? Consider:

Other than family and church, what are the greatest influences in your children's life?

Parade magazine asked teens what influences affected their value systems. In 1960 the greatest influence was parents, then teachers, then friends, then clergy, then counselors, and then popular heroes. In 1980 the same study determined that teens were influenced by: first friends, then parents, then the media (TV, music, movies, etc.). (*Why Knock Rock?* Peters, p. 96)

Peers

Children are born imitators. The desire to conform and be accepted is one of the strongest influences they face. The way other people act, dress, and talk is a powerful force that Satan uses.

1 Corinthians 15:33 – Do not be deceived: "Evil company corrupts good habits." But the fact is that many parents, including Christians, are deceived. We let our children have close friends that are worldly, irreligious, or immoral, yet somehow think our children will escape harm.

Proverbs 13:20 – He who walks with wise men will be wise, but the companion of fools will be destroyed. If our children run with "the wrong crowd," inevitably they and we will suffer the consequences.

Exodus 34:15,16 – One of the strongest areas of peer pressure young people face relates to dating and choosing a marriage companion. Marriage is the closest companionship there is, and dating leads to marriage.

Children of Christians often become too intimate in dating relationships. They face powerful temptations and soon fall into sin. Or they "fall in love" or develop a close relationship with someone who is not a Christian, and soon they compromise truth to please their friend/spouse.

Time and again, Christians have lost their children to Satan through the influence of friends. Do you have a plan for dealing with the influence of your children's friends? How can you raise godly children unless you have a specific, effective plan for dealing with peer pressure?

School

Most of us realize that schools face serious problems. But how serious?

A list of problems faced by children of Christian parents

I once asked a group of teens, who had been raised by Christian parents, to list the problems they faced at school. Here is the substance of their list:

* Lying
* Profanity, dirty jokes, etc. (students and teachers)
* Drinking
* Violence and fighting (students with students or with teachers)
* Immodesty, lack of dress codes
* Coed gym – immodest uniforms
* Smoking
* Peer pressure/bad crowds
* Drugs (7 of 8 students personally knew children who used drugs).
* Ridicule and making fun of children who are good or different
* Gossip, slander
* Cheating
* Stealing and vandalism
* Dancing
* Disrespect for teachers and parents
* False goals (popularity, wealth)
* Classes that justify evolution, abortion, homosexuality, situation ethics, contraceptives, divorce, premarital sex, disrespect for parents, etc.
* Reading assignments with immorality, violence, etc.
* Sexual promiscuity – petting at school, pregnant girls, children talking openly about sexual relations, everyone expected to do it, etc.
* Schedule conflicts with church activities

Some problems in northern Illinois schools

In July, 2010, Teri Paulson from the Illinois Family Institute reported the following problems in area schools:

* She saw posters on the walls of her son's high school social studies teacher (District 211): one of **Malcolm X**, three of **Che Guevara**, and one of **Chairman Mao**. There were no posters of conservative men or women.
* Glenbrook North High School spring musical had a cast of characters that included a gay drag queen, a stripper, and a bi-sexual performance artist.
* Wheeling High School student newspaper featured an article that declared oral sex to be the "new romantic norm" for casual dating.
* Deerfield High School has a mandatory Freshman Advisory class in which homosexual, bi-sexual, and transgender upperclassmen discuss their sexual attractions with freshmen.

* Students in Glenbard North health classes were given a survey, which asked them how they knew they were heterosexual if they had never had a good same-sex lover?

* *Beloved* is required reading in many junior and senior English classes. The very first chapter contains multiple references to men engaging in sexual activity with cows.

* *The Perks of Being a Wallflower* is about the 'perks' of being a voyeur to lots of teenagers having lots of sex. It is taught in many Illinois high schools.

* Deerfield and Highland Park High Schools taught *Angels in America: A Gay Fantasia on National Themes* whose cast of characters includes a black, homosexual, drag queen nurse with a heart of gold, and an Angel whose 'activities' would cause a porn star to blush.

Admittedly, these are extreme examples, but consider what kind of teachers and administrators would even allow such materials, let alone require them. What kind of environment would such schools be? Can your children face such environments 8 or 9 hours a day for half the days of the year for 13 or more of the most impressionable years of their lives without consequence?

All the passages we studied about evil influences apply to these situations. If "evil companions corrupt good morals," how can impressionable children face such an environment and maintain godliness unless you have a plan for fighting these evils?

Entertainment: Television, movies, music, the Internet, and computer games

Would you want your child to spend several hours every day with good friends who continually attempted to persuade your child to accept all the following practices?

* Drug and alcohol abuse
* The occult – witchcraft, Satanism, astrology, sorcery, etc.
* Oriental religions – Hinduism, Buddhism, reincarnation, etc.
* Violence, murder, suicide
* Sexual promiscuity – fornication, adultery, homosexuality, immodesty, and even nudity
* Profanity, cursing, obscenity
* Rebellion against parents, government, God and the Bible

If "running with a bad crowd" can corrupt your child's good morals, how can they not be influenced by close relationships with such evils? Yet, many children of Christians have friends who are just like we have described. Consider just a few of those friends:

Television

The average American watches TV 50 hours per week – ten hours more than the average workweek. *(Bennett, p. 20)*

A study of 58 hours of prime-time TV revealed: 5 rapes, 7 homosexual acts, 28 acts of prostitution, 41 examples of sexual relations between unmarried people. But this study was in 1983! (*Christian Inquirer*, 7 and 8/83)

It has been estimated that, by the time the average child reaches age 18, he will have witnessed more than 15,000 murders on TV or in movies. (Bennett, p. 20)

In 1991 the National Coalition on Television Violence estimated that, if TV violence had never been introduced, each year the US would have 10,000 fewer murders, 70,000 fewer rapes, 1,000,000 fewer motor vehicle thefts, 2,500,000 fewer burglaries, and 10,000,000 fewer acts of larceny. Crime rates would be half what they are now. (Via *Gospel Anchor*, 8/91, p. 17)

A study by the Rand Corp. reported in 2008 that pregnancies were twice as common among adolescents who watched sexualized programs regularly. The study's lead author said, "Our findings suggest that television may play a significant role in the high rates of teenage pregnancy in the United States."

Movies

Many Christians think nothing of letting children attend PG or PG-13 movies. Here is a survey of the contents of PG and PG-13 movies in 1988:

Nearly 1/4 have the "f-word."

61% take God's name in vain.

71% contain vulgar references to excretion, intercourse, or genitals.

50% imply sexual intercourse.

13% show intercourse.

30% show explicit nudity.

75% include moderate or severe violence.

74% depict alcohol or drug abuse (via *Citizen*, 1/89)

In 1992 *Newsweek* reported a survey of moral views of 104 top TV writers and executives. Here are the results compared to the views of the average American (and we have added the views of faithful Christians):

* Believe that adultery is wrong: Hollywood 45%, Americans in general 85%, (Christians 100%).

* Believe homosexual acts are wrong: Hollywood 20%, Americans 76%, (Christians 100%).

* Believe in a woman's right to an abortion: Hollywood 97%, Americans 59%, (Christians 0%).

* Have no religious affiliation: Hollywood 45%, Americans 4%, (Christians 0%). (Via *Citizen*, 9/21/92)

No wonder movies and TV are ungodly!

Modern music

On the average, "teens listen to 10,500 hours of [music] between 7-12 grades ... just 500 hours less than the total time they spend in school over 12 years" (*US News and World Report*, 10/28/85, pages 46-49; via. Gary Fiscus). Consider the problems in modern music:

* Drugs

"...the rock scene is permeated by the values and practices of the drug culture. ... Since the [mid-sixties] many rock lyrics have had drug overtones.

"Rock concerts pose an additional problem ... In many cities, drugs are sold and used openly at these concerts; no real attempt is made to enforce either the drug or the alcohol laws. Rest rooms in public concert halls are often cluttered with children as young as 11 who are getting high, vomiting, or shaking from unpredictable drug and alcohol effects. Most parents are unaware of all this" (*Parents, Peers, and Pot*, Marsha Manatt, US Dept. of Health and Human Services, pages 24,25).

* Violence

Surveys by the National Coalition on Television Violence reveal that over 50% of rock videos feature or suggest violence. ("Violent Videos: a Close Look at MTV," Miller, *Christianity*, 4/85, p. 24). One coalition survey revealed that MTV (music video channel) showed an average of 18 violent incidents per hour (Peters, p. 40).

* Sexual immorality

Consider the following quotes from rock music magazines and performers:

"The surest shortcut to memorable videos seems to be a liberal dose of sex, violence, or both" (*Rolling Stone* Magazine, 12/8/83, p. 76; via Peters, p. 40).

"Everyone takes it for granted rock and roll is synonymous with sex" (Chris Stein of Blondie, *People*, 5/21/79, p. 53; via Peters, p. 107).

Rock and roll is "99 percent sex" (John Oates, *Circus*, 1/31/76, p. 39; via Peters, p. 108).

"Rock and Roll is about sex, and I'm here to corrupt the youth of America" (Elvis Costello, *AFA Journal*, 11&12/88, p. 20).

* Alienation from parents

A Jefferson Starship member said, "our music is intended to broaden the generation gap [and] alienate children from their parents" (Peters, p. 105).

Malcom McClaren: "Rock N' Roll is pagan and primitive and very jungle and that's how it should be. The moment it stops being those things it's dead. ... The true meaning of rock ... is sex, subversion and style" (*Rock* magazine, 8/83, p 60; via Peters, p. 107).

Alfred Arnowitz, former music critic for New York *Post*: "If the establishment knew what today's popular music really is saying, not what the words are saying, but what the music itself is saying, then they wouldn't just turn thumbs down on it, they'd ban it, they'd smash all the records and they'd arrest anyone who tried to play it" (*Searching the Scriptures*, 11/85, p. 540).

The point is not that just one kind of music is dangerous. The point is: do you honestly believe you can raise godly children without a plan for fighting such influences as this?

The Internet and video games

Surely, it should not take much imagination to realize that what we have just said about the above entertainment is as great or greater a danger on the Internet and video games.

If you know anything about the Internet, including email and social networking, you know it is just like any other form of communication: it has good material along with tons of filth. It often reeks with pornography, filthy language, violence, and the Occult, besides rotten concepts.

The special problem is that these evils come right into your home and are so difficult to control. If your children have access to the Internet and email, controlling what they view is extremely difficult. How can you control it if you don't understand it and don't have a plan?

Video games can be especially dangerous because players become active participants in the events they watch. They may pull the trigger to shoot people, they may role-play evil characters, they may use witchcraft and other occult powers to achieve goals. Yet, Satan always disguises evil as good, so participants become desensitized to participating in evil.

If you would not just allow your children to run with any peer group of their choosing, then why allow them to watch TV or movies or listen to music or access the Internet or video games without a plan for supervising them?

The point is not that raising godly children is impossible. It can be done, but no parent will succeed without an effective plan for dealing with these influences.

Developing a Good Plan

How do we develop a good plan? Where do we go for guidance? Many people think it is impossible to know the best way to raise children. Can we *know* the best way?

We Must Not Rely on Human Theories.

Many parents follow human authorities.

Many parents follow advice from so-called experts: psychologists, sociologists, government officials, social agencies, and other child-raising experts.

Other parents just raise their children the way their own parents raised them. This may be done knowingly or more often unknowingly. We just naturally act according to what we are familiar with: we treat our children the way we saw our parents act. This amounts to accepting our own parents as the best authority for how to raise children.

Notice that these are all human authorities. Humans are fallible and often make mistakes, so it is reasonable that many of their theories do not work. This is especially true if our goal is to raise *godly* children.

Remember the Bible warnings about following human authority.

Proverbs 14:12 – There is a way that seems right to a man, but its end is the way of death.

Jeremiah 10:23 – The way of man is not in himself; it is not in man who walks to direct his own steps. No man is as wise as God; so no one knows how to please God by human wisdom, including child-raising experts. People, who don't follow God's guidance, cannot tell us how to raise godly children.

1 Corinthians 1:19-21; 2:4,5 – In matters of godliness and righteousness, we must follow divine wisdom, not human wisdom. This does not mean human advice is always wrong. Sometimes people give advice that agrees with the Bible. But advice that disagrees with the Bible is always wrong!

Christians generally know we must not follow human authority regarding worship, salvation, the church, etc. But raising children is a God-given obligation just as surely as are these other areas. When human ideas differ from God's word, we have no more right to follow them in raising children than in any of these other areas.

We are at war with forces of evil that lead people astray from God's will both in the church and in the home. We can no more defeat the forces of evil by following human wisdom in the home than we can in the church!

(Matthew 15:9,13; Galatians 1:8,9; 2 John 9-11; Colossians 3:17; Proverbs 3:5,6; Revelation 22:18,19; 1 Timothy 1:3; 2 Timothy 1:13)

The Bible Is God's Guide for Raising Godly Children.

2 Timothy 3:16,17 – Raising godly children is a good work, and the Scriptures instruct us in righteousness and equip us for good works.

Joshua 1:8 – Joshua prospered in God's work God when he followed God's word, not departing to the right or left. Likewise, we prosper in the work God gives us if we follow His word.

The Scriptures often compare God's relationship to His children to a father's relationship to his earthly children (Matthew 7:9-11; Hebrews 12:5-11). This is why the term "father" is used both for God and for an earthly parent. It follows that parents can learn many things about our role by observing the example of God our Father in His dealings with us. We will often use His example as a source of guidance in these studies.

Makers of cars and appliances provide their customers with operator's manuals to show how to use the equipment successfully. So, the Maker of the family has given us an instruction book for the family. Does it make sense to follow the ideas of fallible humans, rather than the wisdom of the all-wise God who created families?

Philippians 4:13 – I can do all things through Christ who strengthens me. We do not need to be constantly confused about how to raise children. We can have the strength and guidance we need, but not through human wisdom. We must turn to Jesus.

(Deuteronomy 18:18-22; Psalm 19:7-9; 33:4; 119:128,142,160; John 17:17; Titus 1:2,3; Revelation 19:9; 21:5)

Observe and Learn from Winning Parents

While the Bible is the standard, other people who follow that standard can help us learn it.

Hebrews 6:12 – Imitate those who through faith and patience inherit the promises.

Titus 2:3-5 – Older women should teach the younger women how to love their children and be homemakers.

Titus 2:7 – In all things show yourself a pattern of good works.

As a parent, it won't take you long to realize that lots of people are glad to give you advice about raising children. Many will advise: don't be so strict, spanking won't work, educate your children the way society says to educate them, etc. But Karen and I observed years ago that very few – even among Christians – were themselves doing a really good job with their own children. Their kids did not act the way we wanted our kids to act.

So, before you accept advice, first evaluate it by God's standard. And then ask how successful these people have been with their own children. Are their children obedient and respectful? Do their children know God's will, become Christians when they become accountable, and live faithful Christian lives? In short, do you see evidence that their children are turning out the way you want yours to?

The parents to imitate are those who are successful, not those who fail!

Father and Mother Should Discuss Their Plan and Agree.

Both the father and the mother must be involved in raising the children.

Ephesians 6:4 – Fathers must bring up children in the nurture and admonition of the Lord.

Ephesians 6:1 – Children should be obedient to both parents.

Proverbs 1:8 – Mothers also have authority over their children.

To achieve their goal as parents and to avoid provoking children to discouragement, father and mother must work together. Family rules must be consistent. This requires discussion and agreement.

The best time to make these plans is before problems arise. A couple should discuss their principles and beliefs about child raising even before they marry. Then they should continue to talk about what their rules will be and how they will handle problems. Then when specific problems arise, they can handle them quickly and confidently.

The Plan Must Be Accompanied by Prayer.

James 1:5 – We need to pray for wisdom. This wisdom will come as we study God's word. But we must diligently pray that we will be able to apply His word properly. (Hebrews 5:14)

1 Chronicles 29:19 – David prayed for God to give his son Solomon a loyal heart to keep God's commandments. All parents need to pray every day for each of their children by name, and ask God to strengthen them.

A young man who had gotten into serious trouble was asked about his upbringing. One thing he said was, "I can't remember ever hearing my parents pray for me."

You can learn from my mistake here. All my married life I have prayed every day for my wife and each of my children by name; but when I led a prayer I would never name the people who were present. Why not?

Nearly every letter Paul wrote, he told the people he addressed that he was praying for them. Surely our children deserve at least that much from us. Your children need to know that you name them in prayer.

Do you have a plan for raising your children, a plan based on God's word and prayer?

Conclusion

Too many parents let their own children manipulate them. "I just don't know what to do with them." We need to learn to out-think our children. Our duty as parents requires us to study God's word and apply it so we know how to raise godly children.

The Devil often defeats us, not because it is impossible for us to defeat him, but because *we are not fighting him effectively*. Either we are not aware of the danger, or else we are simply too indifferent to fight. By the time we realize our mistake, it is often too late. But we can win the battle, if we follow God's will and prayerfully develop a plan based on Bible principles.

For each child, you only have one chance to raise that child properly. And before you know it, your kids will be grown. It will be too late then to go back and start over if you haven't done it right. To succeed, we need a plan based, not on human wisdom, but on prayerful study and application of God's will.

Do you have a plan for raising your children? Is your plan based on God's word? How often do you discuss with your spouse the principles on which you act? How diligent are you in your effort to fight Satan and his evil influences on your children?

Key #3: Love

The basis of any good relationship is love, because love leads us to seek the well being of others and do what is best for others (1 Corinthians 13:4,5). Love is not always easy and pleasant; we will see that sometimes parents need "tough love."

Let us consider what love leads parents to **do** and what it leads them to **not** do.

Begin by Loving One Another.

To have a loving family, husband and wife need to start by loving one another.

Love Enough to Stay Together.

Matthew 19:9 – Surely love should lead parents to be faithful to their marriage covenant. God allows only one grounds for divorce. Married couples should not want their marriage to end, nor should they threaten to divorce. Children deserve the security of knowing their home will always be there.

Modern hedonistic society defends divorce by saying children will soon get over it, and they may be better off. Sometimes parents think, "I can't make my children happy if I'm not happy, but I'll never be happy in this marriage." But such ideas are not love; they are selfishness!

Divorce is incredibly traumatic to children, leaving scars for life. People in troubled marriages do not need divorce; they need to learn to get along!

Love Enough to Learn to Treat One Another Right.

Staying together isn't enough; parents also need to love and treat one another right.

Ephesians 5:25,28,29,33 – The husband must love his wife as Christ loved the church and as he loves himself. Love her enough to provide for her, cherish her, and care for her as surely as you do for yourself.

Titus 2:4,5 – Young women should learn to love their husbands and children. Love for children is associated with love for one's spouse. In fact, you cannot truly do one without the other.

Notice that these passages teach that love can be learned. Biblical love is not always romantic and does not always come naturally. Parents should have a natural affection toward one another and toward their children, but natural attraction alone does not always lead us to do what is best. Biblical love leads us to learn God's will for the family, then it motivates us to do it.

Do you love your wife/husband? If not, you need to repent and learn to love by always choosing to do what is best for your spouse.

Love Enough to Show Affection.

1 Corinthians 7:3-5 – Husband and wife should not deprive one another but give "the affection due" to one another. Context shows this includes especially sexual love, but there is a lot more to affection than that. Husband and wife need to speak and act affectionately. Intimacy should be kept private, but children should never doubt that their parents love one another.

Many children say, "I've never seen my parents hug and kiss." Or, "I've never heard my parents say they love one another." Why not? Would your children say that?

Did you hug and hold hands and say "I love you" when you were first married? Then what's so hard about it now? If you love one another, then say so and show it! Your spouse needs to know it and your children need to know it.

Children need to be raised in an atmosphere of love and good will. A pattern of fussing and fighting between parents leads to insecurity and fear for the children. And often the children will imitate that disruptive behavior in their own families when they marry. But if parents establish a pattern of expressing affection, children have a sense of security and they learn the importance of showing affection in their own families.

The first and most basic aspect of love that any parents need is to learn to love one another. Their love for the children should follow from this.

Encourage Children
Whenever Possible.

Colossians 3:21 says not to provoke our children to discouragement. Just as love leads us to do good toward our spouse, it should also lead us to do good for our children.

There is danger that we might be too lax and not require proper obedience. But there is also danger that we may belittle a child till we make him feel worthless. Consider some specifics.

Avoid Humor that Frustrates, Discourages, or Angers.

This is another lesson I have struggled to learn all my life. Humor is good, and can be valuable in dealing with children. But humor is good only if everyone enjoys it and no one gets hurt. Humor that hurts other people's feelings is poor humor and violates the principle of love.

And remember that children are more sensitive at certain ages than at other ages. Things that may not bother adults or other children, may really hurt a particular child at certain stages.

Avoid Belittling Childish Mistakes.

This especially hurts a child when done in the presence of others and most especially in front of his friends. If a mistake needs correcting, do it in a way that shows the child you still love him.

In an episode of "Leave It to Beaver," the father Ward scolded his teenage son Wally for using his father's shaver. Wally needed to be rebuked, but the problem was that Ward did it in front of Wally's friend Eddie Haskel. As a result, Wally ended up being ridiculed by all his school friends.

Don't bring up a child's past mistakes and embarrass him in the presence of others. If the child can genuinely join in the humor, fine. But if you discourage him and make him feel inferior, what good have you accomplished?

Set Your Expectations Within Reach
of the Child's Ability.

Too many parents expect achievement that is simply beyond the child at his best. They may demand things the child can't accomplish till he is older. Others compare one child to other children who may simply possess abilities this child lacks. ("Susie got straight 'A's,' why can't you?")

Express Appreciation for Accomplishments.

Some parents constantly criticize, but rarely praise. We should challenge children to do their best, but many abilities just develop later in life than many parents expect. If a child makes a sincere effort but receives only criticism without praise, he will become discouraged and quit trying: "What's the use? I'll never please them anyway."

Read Colossians 3:21 again.

We should not build our lives around our children or grant their every whim. But neither should we break their spirit by ignoring their feelings.

Do you treat your children in a way that makes them feel they are loved and appreciated?

Determine Rules and Punishments for the Child's Good.

Make Rules for the Good of the Whole Group.

Children sometimes think that being a parent means you get to do whatever you want.

1 Corinthians 13:3 – Love does not seek its own; it is not selfish. Love motivates us to do, not what we want, but what is best for the whole group.

One of the surest ways parents discourage children (Colossians 3:21) is by acting selfishly and unjustly, using their authority unreasonably for their own pleasure. This does not mean the child should just have his way: that is not good for him or for anyone in the group. There must be rules, and rules must be enforced. But they must be made for the good of all.

Exercise Punishment for the Good of the Child.

Some "authorities" claim that all punishment is inherently unloving. *The Complete Book of Mothercraft* says that, whenever punishment occurs, parents have forsaken "the positive feelings of love and understanding" (via *Plain Truth about Child Rearing*, p. 58). Instead, godly parents learn how love and discipline work together.

Hebrews 12:5-11 – God's chastisement of His people illustrates a father's discipline of his children. God chastens those He loves. This is for our profit and yields good fruit. Properly done, chastening is an act of love that benefits those who receive it.

Proverbs 13:24 – He who spares the rod hates his son. One who loves will chasten (use the rod) when needed. (Compare Proverbs 23:13,14.)

The child needs to learn to act properly and respect authority. This will give him a much better life as an adult. We will discuss spanking and punishment later, but the point here is to remember to punish in love for the child's good.

Consider Some Specific Guidelines about Rules, Punishments, and Love.

These involve personal judgment but are generally valid.

Never use your authority to get personal vengeance on a child.

Sometimes parents punish simply because the child inconvenienced or embarrassed them. For example, suppose the child interrupts the parent from a pleasant activity or uses a bad word in front of the parent's friends. The child may need to be punished, but are we motivated by concern for the child, or are we acting from selfish reasons?

Never punish the child in a fit of uncontrolled anger.

Not all anger is sinful, nor it is wrong to punish a child in anger. God has often punished people in anger. But anger must be controlled (Ephesians 4:26).

Sometimes parents beat a child in a fit of rage. Others scream, clench their teeth, and lose control. Such conduct rarely leads to the child's good.

Usually the solution is to punish the child **before** the parent loses his temper, while he is still in control.

Never use authority just to satisfy a desire for power.

Some parents dominate children just to prove that they are boss, to satisfy their ego, or to impress their friends. Like tyrants or dictators, they get a thrill from controlling others.

All such conduct violates God's law of love, unnecessarily discourages children, and leads children to be disrespectful and disobedient.

When you make rules or punish your child, do you act in love for your child's good?

Willingly Sacrifice for the Children's Good.

Sacrifice and giving of ourselves are essential elements of Biblical love.

John 3:16 – God gave His Son because He loves us.

Luke 10:25-37 – The good Samaritan illustrated love by giving time, effort, and money for the well being of another.

1 John 3:16-18 – We imitate Jesus' example, not just by professing love, but by giving what others need.

Children Need Our Time and Attention.

Parents often neglect their children.

Many families rarely play together, work together, worship and pray together, and may not even eat together. Children are often left unattended ("latch-key children"), roam the neighborhood, or go to daycare or babysitters day after day, simply because the parents are busy doing other things. Children often misbehave just to get attention. Others never serve God faithfully because their parents never took the time to teach them God's ways.

Fathers specifically should take time for their children.

Fathers are often too wrapped up in jobs or personal interests. We must provide a livable income (1 Timothy 5:8). But remember, the goal is to raise godly children. What does it profit to provide material things, if our children do not grow up to serve God faithfully (Matthew 16:26)?

Fathers should make sure that the whole family eats at least one meal together (preferably more) every day. They should take time to play, study, and work with their children.

Many fathers realize too late that their priorities were wrong, but by then the children are gone and it is too late to establish a relationship with them. What sacrifices are you making to give your children the time and attention they need?

Specifically, Children Need a Full-time Mother.

This is God's plan, and anything less is less than satisfactory. Granted there may be emergencies where the father is unavoidably unable to provide even basic necessities, and the mother may need to leave the home temporarily to help out. But this is never a good situation and should be changed as soon as possible.

Psalm 113:9

God blesses a woman by giving her a home and making her a joyful mother of children. Motherhood is a cause for joy. Praise God for it! No profession is more valuable or more fulfilling. Yes, it is frustrating and tedious at times, but so is man's work.

1 Timothy 5:14

Young widows should marry, bear children, and guide the house. Woman was created to protect unborn children, give them birth, and then nourish them. This creates a unique bond between mother and child that no one else can ever replace. She is uniquely suited both physically and emotionally for the care of children. When she marries and has children, her work is at home caring for her family.

Feminists, who don't believe the Bible, often argue that children won't suffer if the mother leaves to take a job away from home. Yet often the result is that children spend many hours unattended or at daycare. And then when mother is home, she is too tired or too busy catching up on housework to spend time with the children.

Titus 2:4,5

Young women should be taught to love their husbands and children and be "workers at home" (ASV), "homemakers" (NKJV), "keepers at home" (KJV), "working at home" (ESV). The mother's work is "at home," and her work is to keep or care for the home (family). Note that her care for her family (verse 5) should be motivated by love (verse 4). Her family needs her time and attention, and she thereby fulfills the purpose for her creation.

Many Bible examples show men working away from home to provide family income: carpenters, shepherds, farmers, physicians, fishermen, etc. But the mother's work is at home caring for the family. There is simply no one who can fully replace her.

Look at the list of responsibilities God gives to wives and mothers in verses 4,5. Question: How many of these responsibilities may a woman hire someone else to do in her place while she chooses to do something else instead? May she hire someone else to love her husband, be discreet, chaste, or obedient to her husband? The idea is absurd!

We may pay people to provide assistance by doing some specific task under our supervision (cleaning a room or provide health care or some specific instruction). But why have many come to believe that a woman may hire other people to take over the supervision of her household or the care of her children hour after hour, day after day, while she chooses to work a secular job? Who can honestly believe that is what God intended when He inspired this passage?

John 10:11-14

Jesus contrasts a hireling to a shepherd who owns the sheep. The owner will give his life for the sheep, because he cares for them. But the hireling will not make the same sacrifices, because he does not have the same commitment to the sheep.

Note the principle: a hireling gives inferior care and inadequate sacrifice, because the sheep do not belong to him. If this applies to sheep, how much more so to children? In Matthew 12:12 Jesus asked: "Of how much more value then is a man (child) than a sheep?" **To hire other people to raise children in the parents' place puts the children under inferior care.** No babysitter or daycare center can have the natural attachment that the children's own mother ought to have. If a woman chooses to put her children under inferior care while she does some other job, how can that be harmonized with the Biblical concept of love?

Again, there may be emergencies where the father is incapacitated or otherwise unable to provide. But isn't it true that many mothers simply **choose** to work away from home, while others care for their children? Doesn't this often mean that children do not receive the training and instruction they need, many develop serious moral problems, and many simply never do serve God faithfully? Isn't this a major cause of family problems in our society?

Parents simply must realize that raising children takes much time – quantity time and "quality" time – to be with them and teach them. They must know that we are available when they need us. This requires parents to love their children enough to make sacrifices of time and of material prosperity. (See also Proverbs 31:27; 7:11.)

Learn to Show Affection to Children.

Families of Christian should be affectionate. This also can and should be learned.

Appreciate Our Children as Blessings from God.

Genesis 33:5 – Jacob stated that God had graciously given him his children.

Psalm 127:3-5 – Children are a heritage from the Lord. A man who has his quiver full is happy. Yet, some act like caring for children is unbearable drudgery. We grumble and complain every time we have to do something for them.

Psalm 128:3,4 – Children around our table are a blessing from God. Is this how we feel? Some people obviously don't appreciate their children: they abuse them, desert them, leave them to die, give them away, or murder them before they are even born.

We need to improve our attitude toward children. Let there be no "unwanted children," not because we have murdered them as pro-abortion advocates suggest, but because we have learned to love and appreciate them (Titus 2:4).

How often do you really thank God for your children? Do you view them as a blessing or a burden? Do you act like you appreciate them?

Show Affection by Words and by Physical Contact.

Children have deep emotional needs that are met only when their parents say they love them and then show that they really mean it.

Fathers especially need to learn to express love.

Men tend to think it is effeminate to show love. This was another of my mistakes.

My father was not particularly affectionate. His mother died when he was young and he grew up living with other families. The most affection I remember him showing when I was little was "whiskering" me. As a teenager, I did not want to show affection for others.

Karen's family is affectionate. They hug when they greet and say goodbye. Sometimes the women cry. It took a while, but I now know their way is best.

Every person has a fundamental need for security and a sense of belonging. If this need isn't met in the home, children will seek it elsewhere such as among peers. Boys may join gangs. Girls may become sexually promiscuous to find acceptance from a guy.

Parents, hug and kiss your kids. Tell them you love them.

Do it often every day! This includes your teenage boys!

* Is our Heavenly Father a good example? He frequently assures us, both by deed and by word, that He loves us.

* Genesis 33:4 – When the brothers Jacob and Esau met after a long separation, they embraced, kissed, and wept.

* Genesis 45:15; 46:29 – Joseph embraced, kissed, and wept with his brothers and father.

* Genesis 48:10 – Jacob kissed and embraced Joseph's sons.

* 1 Kings 19:20 – As a grown man Elisha kissed his father and mother goodbye.

* Luke 15:20 – When the prodigal son returned, his father embraced and kissed him.

* Romans 12:15 – Rejoice with those who rejoice and weep with those who weep.

Are these examples somehow unmanly? Is this "corny"? Is it "mush" as Grumpy says in Snow White and the Seven Dwarfs? No, it meets a basic need.

The superintendent of a home for juvenile delinquents said, "Love is a major need of these boys. Their parents will give them a car, but won't say, 'I love you.'" (Webb, p. 125) Some families meet physical needs but neglect emotional needs.

Families should learn to be affectionate both in words and in touch. It begins with snuggling and holding the babies and nursing them the natural way when possible. As they grow it may include hugging, telling them we love them, putting an arm around them, holding hands during prayer, having group hugs, and sympathizing in times of trouble and rejoicing together in times of happiness. It includes remembering special days (birthdays, anniversaries) and giving gifts.

Security, belonging, and closeness are needs children have, just as surely as physical needs. To whom did God give the duty to take the lead to see that family needs are met? It is the duty of the father as the leader and provider (1 Timothy 5:8).

If your parents were not affectionate, you can and should change it in your family. This affection should include all the family members, including the men and boys. Should your family learn to be more affectionate?

(Genesis 27:26,27; Exodus 4:27; 18:7)

Reassurances of love are especially important after we have punished a child.

The child must understand that we object to his conduct, but we do not reject him. This becomes clear if, after punishing the child, we take time to hold him on our lap, talk to him, and then include him in other activities. Don't make him feel an outcast, but assure him of forgiveness (provided he is truly penitent).

We have our children for only a short time. Won't it be a shame, in our old age, if we must look back with regret because our children grew up and left home before we took the time to show them that we care?

Conclusion

1 Corinthians 13:13 – Now abide faith, hope, and love, these three; but the greatest of these is love. Is your family characterized by love?

Key #4: Instruction

Many Scriptures tell parents to teach and guide their children. This includes many aspects of life, but we must especially teach children the word of God and its application. Children, in turn, should heed this instruction.

Proverbs 1:8 – Sons should hear the instruction of their fathers and not forsake the law of their mothers.

Psalm 34:11 – David determined to teach future generations the fear of the Lord.

Isaiah 38:19 – The father shall make known God's truth to the children.

2 Timothy 3:15 – From childhood Timothy had been taught the Scriptures because they could make him wise to salvation.

Consider some principles involved in instructing children. As we do so, notice the many other passages that show the importance of instructing children.

(Compare 1 Thessalonians 2:11; Ephesians 6:4.)

How Should We Instruct Children?

What methods should we use to instill God's word in our children?

Word of Mouth

Genesis 18:19 – Abraham commanded his family after him what to do to serve God.

Deuteronomy 4:9,10 – The things the parents know should be made known to the children.

Psalm 78:4-8 – Tell God's law to the next generation so they know it and tell their children.

Parents must take time to talk to children about God's word. Explain the teachings and the principles involved. Discuss with them, ask them questions, and answer their questions.

How diligently do you teach God's word to your children? How well do they know the truth?

(See also Deuteronomy 6:6-9; Psalm 48:13; 71:18; etc.)

Example

We all learn by imitation. We learn new jobs by watching others do them, etc. Children especially learn by mimicking. Toddlers want to wear our shoes and clothes, talk like us, etc.

So, children need to *see* their parents living by Bible principles. But remember that they imitate both good and bad characteristics.

2 Timothy 1:5 – Timothy's genuine faith was first possessed by his mother and his grandmother. They not only told Timothy what to believe, they showed him by their own faith. "Actions speak louder than words."

Ezekiel 16:44 – "Like mother, like daughter." Most parents want their children to live better than they themselves have lived, but this is rare. The general rule is that children are like their parents. If our children are no better than we are, what will they be like?

1 Kings 15:3 – Abijam walked in the sins of his father. Many such statements can be found regarding kings of Israel and Judah. Children often imitate their parents' sins.

And children often go further in justifying sin than their parents do. We knew a family in the church where the kids grew up hearing the father argue that there isn't anything wrong with drinking a beer now and then. His kids ended up leading the church's teens in drinking parties; one of his sons became so drunk at one party he vomited. Parental example is important.

Genesis 27 and 37 – Isaac and Rebekah played favorites with their children, and Rebekah influenced Jacob to deceive Isaac. When Jacob had children, he in turn played favorites, and his sons in turn deceived him. When you practice evil, you may as well expect your children to practice it too – and they will probably practice it toward you!

Are there things about your life that you don't want your children to imitate? If so, you need to change it now! Woe to us if, by our example, our children are lost eternally. It would be better for us to be drowned than to suffer the fate we will suffer in such a case (Matthew 18:6,7).

If your children imitate you, will they lie, deceive, smoke, drink, gamble, dress immodestly, neglect the Lord and the church? Or will they be honest, hard working, and diligent in Bible study, prayer, teaching God's word to others, and working in the church?

(Nehemiah 13:23,24; Matthew 23:1-4)

Practice

Usually people learn best, not just by being told what to do, nor even by watching others, but by actually practicing the activity guided by an instructor. This is how most people learn to play the piano, drive a car, or participate in a sport, etc.

Parents need to teach their children to work by having them help you work: housework, gardening, making repairs, and work of all kinds. But especially children should learn to serve God by practicing it under their parents' guidance.

Hebrews 5:14 – To discern good and evil, senses must be exercised by reason of *use* (NKJV footnote: "practice"). It is not enough just to speak truth to children, nor even to set a good example before them. We must also insist that they regularly practice what is right. This will instill in them the *habit* of doing right, so they will continue to be faithful throughout life.

Do you insist that your children practice what you teach them till it becomes a way of life with them? In later lessons we will discuss **how** to get children to practice what we teach them. The point here is proper instruction requires that children, not just see and hear from others what it right, but themselves practice what is right.

Repetition

Humans are creatures of habit, and habits develop by repetition. So all these teaching methods need frequent repetition: telling, good example, and especially practicing what is right.

Deuteronomy 6:6-9 – Parents should talk continually of God's commands. Write them down where you see them frequently. All this involves repetition and reminder.

2 Peter 1:12-15 – Sometimes young people tire of hearing parents repeat things, but Peter repeatedly reminded people of things they already knew. To do otherwise he said would be "neglect." He knew they would need these lessons after he died.

When children act contrary to what their parents said, one of their most common excuses is, "I forgot." Every time a child uses that excuse, he is admitting the value of reminders! Like Peter, someday your parents will be gone and won't be there to remind you.

Take care that repetition does not become nagging and lecturing. When kids already know something, all they may need is, not a lecture, but just a short reminder. Or ask them to explain the matter to you. But make sure the truth is fresh in their minds.

These methods will instill God's will in your children's minds and ingrain them in their character. What about your children – have they been thoroughly instructed in God's ways?

(Exodus 13:8,14-16)

When and Where Should We Instruct Children?

Deuteronomy 6:6-9 – We should teach continually (walking, sitting, lying, etc.). Consider some specific applications:

Begin Early

A child's character is formed primarily in his early years, so we must begin early to instill God's word.

2 Timothy 3:15 – Timothy knew the Scriptures "from childhood."

Matthew 21:15,16 – Jesus desired praise from babes and nursing infants. God and His will should be among the very first things that children learn. Some of the very first words your children learn should be "God," "Jesus," and "Bible." Let them grow up talking about God.

When children are small, anticipate later problems, and begin to instill habits that will prevent those problems.

Proper training of young children helps them avoid spiritual problems as teenagers. The problems that children have usually begin when they are little, then grow as they grow. When teenage years come, it may be too late to change the child. Don't give up teaching your teens, but the best way to avoid serious problems is to train them properly long before they become teens!

When I was in the fourth grade, the schools taught dancing; but my parents would not let me participate. You might think that a fourth-grader would not be likely to lust. But because my parents started young, dancing was never an issue for me later. But if you let a child dance in grade school, how will you convince him not to go to the proms and high school dances?

The same principle applies in many other areas.

Some people say, "Don't indoctrinate little children. Let them decide for themselves what they believe when they are grown."

Or they say, "I don't think you should make a child go to church or Bible class."

But the truth is, you can't *avoid* indoctrinating a child.

There is no way to be neutral about God (Matthew 12:30). If **you** serve God faithfully, then your child will see and hear you living and teaching God's word. But if you **never** do or say anything about God, then you are teaching the child that God is unimportant. Either way you are teaching the child about religion.

Furthermore, Satan will attempt to indoctrinate your child.

Do you think Satan will wait till the child is grown before he places temptations and false teachings before him? You must begin early to teach the truth, or Satan will win by default!

In a garden, good plants must be cultivated, but weeds grow by themselves. So, we must teach children the truth early, or Satan will fill their lives with spiritual weeds.

So, the fact is that the child will be indoctrinated regardless of what we do or don't do. ***The only question is: What values will he be taught?*** To fail to teach the truth is to guarantee that Satan has a head start, leaving our children defenseless against his lies.

So, the only one who really gains if we don't teach our children early is Satan.

It follows that he is the ultimate source of the view that parents should not indoctrinate children. When you hear people say "don't indoctrinate children," you can be sure they are not faithful Christians. Knowingly or unknowingly, they are tools of Satan.

God knows what children need, and He commands us to teach and to begin early.

Attend ALL Church Assemblies and Classes.

This too should begin early in a child's life.

Bring him from the age he is first able to go anywhere. At first he will not understand what is being said, yet your example will permanently impress him that these meetings are important. Later on, he will learn *why* they are important. (Parents are also learning an important lesson of commitment to God that strengthens them and gives them the assurance they did their best.)

Your child should never be able to remember a time when he did ***not*** attend church meetings regularly.

Regular attendance should be so routine that the whole family automatically knows that everyone will attend every meeting (Hebrews 10:25; Acts 11:26).

This should be a predetermined appointment for every family member. There should be no doubt in any mind where they will be when the church is meeting on Sunday, Bible classes, or gospel meetings.

Less important matters (school activities, sports, musical activities, etc.) should never be allowed to hinder church meetings. That also applies to jobs. Working a job may be good for teens, but they have no God-given obligation to provide for the family like their fathers do. So how can they be justified in missing church for work?

Children should be trained from the beginning to seek first the kingdom and sacrifice for the cause of Christ (Matthew 6:33; Romans 12:1,2).

Parents should make sure all family members come with their lessons prepared.

Parents must set the proper example by having their own lessons prepared. They should also check with teachers from time to time to see how their children are doing. Church meetings and classes are only part of the teaching children need, but the least parents can do is to bring their children to meetings on time and well prepared.

I have sat trying to console parents who were indifferent and irregular regarding attendance in their early marriage, only to find that their children grow up and decide not to attend at all. But by then it is too late for the parents to change them. What a shame!

How regular is your family in attending church meetings?

Have Regular, Organized Studies at Home.

Every child should have daily Bible study at home.

The primary duty for teaching children rests on parents, not on the church. The church can help, but parents need to teach the importance of regular, frequent study at home. Consider:

Acts 17:11 – The Bereans were noble for searching the Scriptures *daily*.

Hebrews 3:13 – To avoid falling away, people need *daily* admonition.

Psalm 1:2; 119:97-99; Joshua 1:8 – We should meditate on God's word *day and night*. (Reread Deuteronomy 6:6-9.)

1 Peter 2:2; Matthew 5:6 – We should hunger and thirst for God's word as a man thirsts for water and as a baby does for milk.

Do these verses describe something to be done just once or twice a week? Parents should teach their children this kind of daily commitment to Bible study.

Much good material is available to help parents in teaching.

Many good books and recordings are available to teach Bible stories to younger children.

Parents can review the children's church Bible class lessons with them at home. You can also order other Bible class material to study with the children at home.

My wife taught our children the books of the Bible by having them say one book for each step, every time they went up or down the stairs together.

A good way to memorize Bible verses is to write them on cards, place the cards on the table, and have everyone say them at meals till the whole family knows them.

For years our family read a chapter of the Bible every evening at the supper table. Then we would go around the table asking one another questions about the chapter.

Many good study methods are available. The point is that parents need to have regular, organized Bible studies to make sure their children learn God's will.

What about your family – are they being thoroughly instructed in God's will?

Teach Informally as Occasions Present Themselves.

Deuteronomy 6:6-9 – Note the emphasis on teaching under all circumstances. We need prearranged studies in which we determine beforehand when and what we will study. But we should also watch for the "teachable" moment that may occur unplanned on the "spur of the moment."

Here are some suggestions about informal teaching.

Promote a relationship of open conversation with children.

Before you can help them apply God's word to their problems, they need to feel free to bring their problems to you.

I made mistakes here too. I am not a good conversationalist, I often thought I had more important things to do, and especially I let my wife become a buffer between my kids and me. If they had requests or concerns, they went to Karen first. If she approved it, she would come to me and defend the kids' case. If I disapproved, she would explain my conclusion to the kids.

The effect was to isolate me from my children. Dad was unapproachable. Mom was the only one the kids could really talk to. And if Mom agreed to something, then by the time it got to Dad, everybody else had already agreed. If Dad vetoed it, then Dad became this gruff ogre, the bad guy. My kids were teenagers before I realized my mistake and tried to correct it.

Some suggestions for open conversation with kids:

Take time to be available from early ages.

If you take time to talk with them when they are little, they are more likely to take time to talk to you when they are older. Do things together as a family and each parent individually with each child. Plan activities together and make use of informal occasions to be together.

This is another problem area if both parents are employed outside the home or spend too much time on outside activities. Opportunities to establish an open relationship are missed.

Often the "generation gap" exists because parents fail to take the time to talk to their kids.

Especially remember the three most important times to be available to your kids: meal times, when they come home from school, and bed time.

Kids are especially talkative at these times. Ask about their activities. Think of topics you can bring up to discuss. Always have at least one meal per day (preferably more than one) as a family and encourage good conversation (not talk for the sake of talk, but constructive conversation).

Do things together as a family.

Read books together as a family. Attend your children's ball games, school functions, and musical performances. Get to know their friends. Listen to music, watch movies, or participate in other entertainment together. Help with their homework. Know what they are involved in, so you can discuss with them.

Honestly listen to them and treat their conversation seriously.

Don't try to do most of the talking. Let them talk so you know what interests them and what they are thinking.

If a problem or viewpoint is serious to them, you should treat it seriously as you would with an adult friend. If you disagree, try to reason at your child's level, but don't ridicule, make fun, or "talk down" to him. Otherwise, next time he won't come to you with his concern.

Ability to talk to your children will lead to the following kinds of teaching opportunities:

Teach when children ask questions.

Many of Jesus' most memorable lessons came in response to questions. This includes the Good Samaritan (Luke 10:29ff), teaching on divorce and remarriage (Matthew 19:3ff), and the discussion of the greatest command (Matthew 22:36ff).

Likewise, children often ask questions that give excellent teaching opportunities: questions about death, prayer, baptism, smoking, etc. When the child asks, he is obviously interested and receptive. Don't just make a brief comment; discuss the matter.

Participate in religious discussions in the child's presence.

Discuss the sermon on the way home from services. Ask each child about his/ her Bible class. Invite visiting preachers or other Christians into your home and have religious discussions.

Don't think children won't learn because "it's over their heads." They will understand more than you think, and later they will remember the importance of these discussions.

And yes, parents should discuss in the children's presence when the church faces problems. I've been familiar with Bible teaching about divorce and remarriage ever since my teen years, because the church dealt with it in my best buddy's family.

Some judgment is needed, but too many parents hide church troubles from their children so the children are shocked when they grow up and must deal with problems. Obviously the children do not need to solve the problems, but they need to grow up knowing there will be problems in the church. Then they can learn from their parents' example how to deal with problems.

Discuss circumstances in life that present good moral lessons.

A temptation a friend faces may make a good lesson about handling temptation. A car wreck may make a good lesson about obeying the law. A Christian who has problems with a non-Christian spouse may teach the importance of marrying a Christian. Many such examples will arise.

As a teenager, I was watching a ball game on TV, when a fight broke out. The camera showed Minnie Minoso calmly sitting on second base, waiting for the game to continue. My mother simply said, "That's what a Christian would do." Obviously, the lesson stuck with me.

Discuss Bible principles when the child faces spiritual decisions or when his conduct is spiritually unacceptable.

Don't just tell your children what your rules are or punish him for disobeying rules. Tell them **why** you made the rule, especially if there are Bible principles involved.

Discuss the principles with the child. Get the Bible out and look up passages together. When he grows up, he won't have you there to tell him right from wrong. But if he understands the principles involved, then he can make right decisions for himself.

Obviously not every decision should be explained. Sometimes there is no time, or the child may be too young to understand. And sometimes children repeatedly demand to know "Why?" even when you have tried repeatedly to explain. They question the explanation simply because they don't like the rule. But within reason, we should explain our reasons as a teaching tool.

Sometimes it may be useful to test our children's understanding of Bible principles by asking them to explain the principles and make the application to a certain situation. Let them reach the conclusion and explain it to you. Give guidance and additional information, if needed. And never let him reach a wrong conclusion. But help him learn to think things through for himself.

Conclusion

I am convinced that most Christians neglect to teach God's word to their children as they ought. Many of us let our children face serious temptations day after day at school, on TV, in music, with friends, etc. In many cases, we simply let them face far too much temptation. But then we make matters worse by neglecting to give them the instruction they need to deal with those temptations. No wonder we are losing so many young people to the world.

When we bring a child into this world, God expects us to instruct that child to do His will. That job belongs to us simply because we are parents, and God will hold us accountable for how well we do the job.

Are ready to give answer to God in judgment for the way we are training our children?

Key #5: Authority (Control)

Authority is the right to give instructions and require obedience.

Our age generally opposes the concept of authority, rules, law, and duty.

People insist on doing their own thing, being their own person, and having their own way. As one man said to me, "I don't want anybody telling me what to do."

So, people demand "freedom" from restrictions. Some object when government is firm with criminals or when schools enforce strict rules toward children. Some object when the church teaches the need for strict obedience to God's laws or when those who disobey are rebuked and disciplined. Some object to the concept of a firm God who hates evil and punishes evildoers!

This rejection of authority is especially obvious in the modern concept of the family. How often do you see TV shows, books, movies, or cartoons that portray a father as a capable, responsible family leader? Generally, either he shares authority equally with the wife, or else he is a bumbler, dominated and manipulated by his wife.

Likewise, society denies that parents should exercise authority over children.

Parent Effectiveness Training, introduced by Thomas Gordon, advocates that parents give up all use of authority. Family conflicts must be resolved by finding a course that is mutually agreeable to both parent and child. Neither is permitted to "impose" his solution on the other. (See the high school text *Parenting and Children*, by H. Westlake, pages 46-50.)

Growing a Godly Marriage

The Children's Liberation Movement leads young people to rebel against parents like the Women's Liberation movement led women to rebel against their husbands.

> We want the power to determine our own destiny. We want the immediate end of adult chauvinism ... Age might once have led to wisdom, but the old have proven themselves unable to deal with present reality ... the young must take the lead... – "Youth Liberation," Youth Liberation Press, via *Christian Inquirer*, 10/79

Child welfare agencies are often staffed by social workers who claim that parents have no right to exercise firm leadership. They may threaten to prosecute parents who exercise authority.

As a result, many children have their own parents "buffaloed." Parents are afraid to be strict, lest their children throw a fit, run away, get into drugs, report them to the government, or are taken away by government agencies. The children, not the parents, end up dominating the home.

Nevertheless, proper use of authority is an essential key to successful parenthood.

Why Is Authority Important in the Home?

God Ordained Authority in the Home.

Husbands have authority over wives.

Ephesians 5:22-24 – The wife should obey her husband as the church should obey Christ. Can the church please God if it disobeys Jesus? No, and neither can the wife please God if she disobeys her husband. This applies in "everything." The only exception would be if her husband required her to sin against God (Acts 5:29).

1 Corinthians 11:3 – The head of the woman is the man, just as the head of man is Christ.

1 Peter 3:1,5,6 – Women should be subject to their husbands as Sarah was to Abraham. (See also Titus 2:5; Colossians 3:18.)

Consider this quotation from Judge Samuel Leibowitz who was a Senior Judge in Brooklyn Criminal Court:

> Young people in Italy respect authority ... That respect starts in the home – then carries over into the school, the city streets, the courts.
>
> I went into Italian homes to see for myself. I found that even in the poorest family the father is respected by the wife and

children as its head. He rules with varying degrees of love and tenderness and firmness. His household has rules to live by, and the child who disobeys them is punished.

Thus I found the nine-word principle that I think can do more for us than all the committees, ordinances and multi-million-dollar programs combined: *Put Father back at the head of the family.*

The American teen-ager has been raised in a household where "obey" is an outlawed word, and where the mother has put herself at the head of the family. – *Reader's Digest*, March, 1958, via *Plain Truth about Child-Rearing*, p. 7

Whether or not this description is still true in Italy, the principle is still true because it agrees with the Bible.

Parents have no basis to expect children to respect their authority, until the parents correct their own relationship toward authority. As it was with love, so it is with authority. To relate properly to the children, parents must begin by relating properly to one another.

Parents have authority over children.

Proverbs 1:8 – A son should hear his father's instruction and not forsake his mother's law.

Ephesians 6:1; Colossians 3:20 – Children should obey their parents.

Luke 2:51 – Jesus set the example for children by being subject to His earthly parents.

Deuteronomy 21:18-21 – The Old Testament said to stone a stubborn and rebellious son, who would not obey his parents.

Romans 1:30,32 – As with other sins listed, those who disobey their parents are worthy of death, and so are those who justify others who disobey.

Isaiah 3:12 – God described evil in Israel, saying that children would oppress them and women would rule over them. The existence of such conditions indicates a decadent society.

These teachings all come from the word of God. God made both parents and children. He knows what is best for all. If these views seem overly strict to us, then we should seriously ask ourselves whether we too have been influenced by our permissive society.

(Compare 2 Timothy 3:2; Jeremiah 35; Philippians 2:22; 1 Peter 1:14; Proverbs 30:17.)

Authority Produces Cooperation and Organization in the Home.

A group of people needs organization and cooperation in order to work together effectively. But organization and cooperation require someone to be recognized as a leader. This explains why God ordained authority in every human relationship that He ordained.

Citizens must submit to civil government

See Romans 13:1-6; 1 Peter 2:13,14.

Imagine what a country would be like if there were no rules. No one would even know what side of the street to drive on or who had the right-of-way at intersections!

Employees must submit to their employers

See Ephesians 6:5-8; 1 Peter 2:18.

Consider what a business would be like with no supervision. How could a company function if everyone came and went as they pleased, or did whatever they pleased whenever they pleased?

So, authority is needed to achieve cooperation. Without leadership, every effort to work together would be ruined due to indecision. Likewise, in the home, someone has to be in charge. God has ordained that the husband is the head, and the children should submit to the parents.

Authority Enables Children to Benefit from the Parents' Wisdom.

By reason of experience, parents generally have more wisdom than children.

Proverbs 29:15 – A child left to himself (unsupervised) will cause shame. But the rod and reproof will give him wisdom (gained from the parents).

Proverbs 4:10-12 – Because of his parents' instructions, the child is wiser. He can avoid problems and mistakes he might otherwise make.

This gives children a sense of security.

Children generally know their parents are wiser than they are. They know they need guidance at times. They may act confident, but behind the false front they are often insecure. Parental guidance assures the child that he is doing what is best. That is why children actually have greater respect for adults who enforce fair rules than they have for permissive parents.

To illustrate, imagine driving in steep mountains and crossing a bridge over a deep chasm – with no guardrails! Would you be afraid? With guardrails, we can be confident, even though we may be just a few feet from the edge. So, the limits set by parents give children security. They know their parents will not let them do anything that would be seriously harmful.

Authority Molds Children's Character and Habits.

Proper training develops character that children will maintain even when older.

Proverbs 22:6 – Properly trained children will not depart from their training even when they are old. People live according to their character and habits. If we train children to develop good character and habits, they will probably maintain those habits. But habits come by repetition. So, parents should insist that children practice what is right till it becomes ingrained.

How can parents get children to practice and develop good habits?

Reasoning with children, by itself, will not always work, even if parents have a good relation with their children. Sometimes the child is simply too young or too rebellious to understand and appreciate our reasons (compare 1 Corinthians 13:11). But if we wait until he understands and agrees with what is right, it may be too late to ingrain the proper habits.

1 Samuel 2:22-25; 3:12,13 – Note that Eli **told** his sons they were wrong – he instructed them. But it wasn't enough. They still would not obey. God rejected Eli's house because Eli did not **restrain** his sons.

What was Eli missing? Authority! He did not make and enforce rules to control his sons and require them to practice good habits and character. Proper control restrains and molds the child's conduct so that good qualities and habits tend to stay with him even when he is mature.

Parental Authority Teaches Children to Respect All Authority.

Adults must regularly relate to all kinds of authority.

As discussed earlier, in government, business, and the home, authority organizes people to work together. If we want to raise children to be well-adjusted adults, we must teach them how to properly relate to authority: how to submit to others who have authority, and how to exercise authority when they themselves have it.

How can we accomplish this? The best way is to develop a proper authority relationship between our children and ourselves. This teaches children how to properly submit to authority, and the parents' example shows children how to properly use authority.

Many "psychologists" teach the opposite. They say use of authority makes children maladjusted, destroys their self-image, and makes them more likely to rebel. So parents think, "I don't want my children to rebel," so they give in to them. The result is manipulation and emotional blackmail. God's word says just the opposite. Does He know best or doesn't He?

The main reason so many children today grow up rebellious and maladjusted is simply that they have **not** been properly required to submit to authority. They manipulate their parents, and the parents don't know what to do about it. They successfully rebel against their parents, so they proceed to rebel against the whole "establishment": government, employers, church, and God. Instead of teaching them submission, we have taught them rebellion by allowing it to "succeed."

The truth is that parents are the primary authorities that children must relate to for their first twenty or so years, and especially for their first five years. If parents allow their children to manipulate them and get their own way against their parents' better judgment – most likely those children will always have difficulty relating to authority and will live a miserable life.

People must especially learn how to relate to the authority of God.

If children do not learn respect for God's authority while at home, they may never learn it.

> When a child can successfully defy his parents during his first fifteen years, laughing in their faces and stubbornly flouting their authority, he develops a natural contempt for them ... His parents are not deserving of his respect, and he does not want to identify with anything they represent ... This factor is important for Christian parents who wish to sell their concept of God to their children. They must first sell themselves. If they are not worthy of respect, then neither is their religion or their morals, or their government, or their country, or any of their values – Dr. James Dobson, *Dare to Discipline*, page 12.

God Himself is an "authority figure." To receive eternal life, we must obey Him (Matthew 28:18-20; 7:21-27; Ecclesiastes 12:13; Hebrews 5:9; 1 Peter 1:22; etc.). But if a child grows up without learning respect for authority – if he develops a pattern of disobeying his parents' rules and getting away with it – he will naturally rebel against God and think he can get away with that!

This is exactly the point where many Christian parents lose their children to the world. This is usually the "bottom line." If you do not restrain your children but let them manipulate you and evade your authority, they will most likely grow up to disrespect God and His will – just like Eli's sons did (1 Samuel 3:13). And God will hold you accountable, like he did Eli.

It follows that parents must learn to properly exercise authority, not for their own benefit, but for the good of the child. Authority teaches lessons that benefit the child both now and for eternity. This is why use of authority is not contrary to love but is a proper exercise of love.

How Should Children Show Respect for Authority?

Some parents don't seem to realize that they have disrespectful children. So, what is included in the respect we seek to teach our children?

Children Must Act Obediently.

This is the essence of respect for authority. Many passages specifically state this.

Ephesians 6:1 – Children obey your parents in the Lord. God says, "This is right"!

Romans 1:30,32 – Those who disobey parents are worthy of death.

In all areas of life, respect for authority requires obedience. So, a child who persistently disobeys in the home is a child who simply has not learned respect for authority. Yet in home after home – even the homes of Christians – children repeatedly refuse to obey. The parent says, "Johnny, do this," but Johnny does what he wants instead. Then the parents apologize for it, laugh it off, or simply ignore it like it's an everyday occurrence.

Parents, you are trying to raise *godly* children. The ultimate goal of your authority is to teach your children respect for *God's* authority. **You should expect your children to obey you like God will expect them to obey Him.** Do they?

Do your children obey promptly, or do they procrastinate, make excuses, manipulate, and evade your instructions? Do they obey with an attitude of good will, or do they groan, complain, whine, make faces, and stomp away? Do they obey exactly, or do they bend the rules and justify partial obedience? Do they obey when you are not watching or only if they know they will get caught? What kind of obedience does God expect of us? If your children have not learned to obey you like they should obey God, then you have work to do. God says it your job to teach them!

(Compare Deuteronomy 21:18-21; 2 Timothy 3:2; Colossians 3:20.)

Children Must Speak Respectfully.

Our permissive age allows children, from preschoolers to teens, to say anything, in any tone of voice, and with any attitude. One high school parenting text says parents should allow "children the right to have all kinds of feelings and wishes and to express them freely" (*Caring for Children*, Draper and Draper, p281). So, your child has the right to say whatever he wants to.

That's why we hear little children yell and scream at parents, mock them, and backtalk ("sass"): "No, I won't! You can't make me! You leave me alone! You shut up!"

We are told this "gets it out of their system." But remember, what we repeatedly practice becomes our habit. What such conduct really does is ingrain the habit of disrespect for authority. It makes rebellion a fundamental part of their "system"!

Consider the teaching of Scripture.

Ephesians 6:2,3 – Children should **honor** their parents. This includes many things, such as supporting the parents in their old age. But one thing included is speaking respectfully.

Matthew 15:4 – Jesus contrasted "honoring" parents to speaking evil of them. He who cursed his parents should "be put to death" under the Old Law (compare Exodus 21:17). To curse means to express a desire for harm to befall someone. Cursing does not necessarily involve using profanity – though we sometimes hear children do that too! Some kids say to their parents, "Oh, drop dead." "Go jump off a bridge." If that isn't cursing, what is it? Is it "honoring" the parent?

Proverbs 30:11,17 – Destruction will come to a son who curses, mocks, or disobeys his parents. Yet, parents often tolerate children who rebelliously make fun of them and disobey them.

1 Timothy 5:1 – Do not rebuke an elder, but exhort him as a father. There are respectful ways to speak to a father, and there are disrespectful ways.

Specifically, parents should never, never let their children say "No" to the parents' rules. This does not refer to when the parent simply asks what the child wants, but when the parent has given the child an instruction. Does saying "No" express honor to the parent? Does it express obedience? May we say "No" to God?

We must tell our kids, "Don't you talk to your mother like that!" And the other parent must back it up. We should train our children to speak respectfully to us, not for our own selfish pride, but because they need to learn respect!

(Compare Ezekiel 2:3-7; 22:7; Exodus 20:12; Leviticus 19:3; Deuteronomy 27:16.)

May a child ever express disagreement with a parent's decision?

Some parents refuse to ever allow a child to express disagreement. This builds rebellion because it is unfair. Such an approach assumes parents are infallible, which is simply untrue.

1 Timothy 5:1 said Timothy could speak to an elder as to a father – including telling him he was wrong. But the manner he did it must be respectful. If a child speaks calmly, but simply thinks he has a better idea or just does not understand the parents' decision, discuss with him. Maybe he does have a better idea. Or if not, the discussion may

help him understand the parents' views. Let the parent consider the child's view, but it must be clear that the child must live with the final decision whether or not he likes it.

But if a child speaks with a rebellious, defiant, disrespectful attitude or tone of voice (parents can tell the difference, and so can children), parents must punish the child's defiance, regardless of the worth of his ideas.

We must teach children that we are willing to discuss if they have a humble, respectful attitude; but rebellion will not be tolerated. (Compare Matthew 19:19; Mark 7:10; 10:19; Luke 18:20.)

Children Must Never Strike or Hit Their Parents.

When a child becomes angry or frustrated, he may strike a parent in anger. Sometimes larger children injure or even murder their parents.

Exodus 21:15 – He who strikes a parent would be put to death under the Old Law. ("Smite" does not necessarily mean to kill – compare verses 18,19).

Proverbs 19:26 – He who does violence to ("assaults" – NASB) his parents is a shame and reproach. (Compare 1 Timothy 1:9.)

Parents must begin early to teach children such conduct will not be tolerated. If your little child hits you in defiance and disagreement with your wishes, you must punish that child severely and teach him he never has the right to strike you.

Some Specific Suggestions for Dealing with Problem Areas

We earlier discussed some of the major forces that often influence young people away from God. Consider some suggestions about using our authority as parents to control these forces.

Entertainment

What should parents do about immoral entertainment: television, movies, music, computer games, the Internet, etc.?

Realize that the nature of our entertainment really does matter.

1 Thessalonians 5:21,22 – Prove all things. Hold fast what is good; abstain from what is evil. God's people must examine what they do and take a stand against evil.

Ephesians 5:11 – Have no fellowship with the unfruitful works of darkness, but rather expose them. If a particular form of entertainment is a work of darkness, may we enjoy it and promote it, or should we oppose it and speak out against it?

Philippians 4:8 – Meditate on things that are true, honorable, just, pure, lovely, etc. Does the entertainment we are considering fall in these categories? If not, why fill our minds with it?

(2 Corinthians 13:5; 1 Peter 5:8,9; 2 Corinthians 6:14-7:1; 1 Timothy 5:22; Deuteronomy 7:25,26; Proverbs 22:3; Romans 12:1,2; Matthew 18:6-9; 1 Corinthians 15:33; Proverbs 13:20; 4:23; Psalm 1:1; 26:5; Proverbs 23:17,20,21; Psalm 101)

Evaluate and correct your own entertainment.

Matthew 7:1-5 – Before we rebuke others, we must correct our own conduct. Are we setting the proper example for our children? Or could it be that the reason they see nothing wrong with immoral entertainment is because of our example? (Matthew 5:16; 18:6,17; 23:1ff; Romans 2:21ff)

Train children from early years to evaluate entertainment, and to enjoy wholesome activities.

Proverbs 22:6 – Train children in the right way so they will continue that way throughout life. When our children are small, if we insist that the family avoid corrupt entertainment, and if we provide wholesome alternatives, children will develop the habit of examining their entertainment, enjoying what is wholesome, and rejecting what is corrupt. If our children learn to enjoy and appreciate what is good, they are far less likely later to enjoy what is corrupt.

Participate as a family and discuss entertainment with your children.

Too often parents and children enjoy different kinds of entertainment, so they just go their separate ways. Parents don't watch TV or play games with their children or listen to their music, so they don't know what their children are involved in.

Ephesians 6:1-4; Proverbs 22:6 – Parents are required to train the children to serve God. We must examine what they do, so we can guide them properly. Sit down together, play their music, play their computer games with them, watch their TV programs, watch movies together, read books together as a family, then evaluate them according to Bible standards.

Avoid allowing unlimited access to TV, radio, computer, etc.

Develop rules so *you* are in control.

Buy, rent, or record video movies, CD's, etc. (these are much easier for parents to control). Preview these with your children. If a song, movie, etc., is unacceptable, tape over it or teach children to turn it off or skip it.

Keep the TV, computer, etc. in family living areas so you can monitor what is done. Do not allow children to have a CD player or radio in their own room until they are old enough and prove themselves to be responsible in using it. Then take it away if they abuse the privilege. Frankly, I doubt they should ever be allowed to have a TV or computer in their own room.

Install child-access controls on the Internet. Use TV-Guardian, Clearplay, or other such controls to eliminate foul language and immorality on TV.

Allow no entertainment that the parents have not specifically previewed and approved. Make sure children know exactly what specific TV programs, tapes, albums, and radio stations are permitted. Try to attend movies as a family. Before allowing any family member to watch a movie, investigate it for profanity, sexual suggestiveness, etc. Check evaluations of movies on sources such as www.screenit.com, www.movieguide.org, and others.

Limit the number of hours per day or week your child may participate. Initiate a system whereby children must work to earn the privilege of enjoying some entertainment. Require all chores and homework to be done first. Do not use TV as a babysitter.

In short, control entertainment with a vengeance! Use the off button! If you cannot control some area, then get rid of it altogether. No entertainment is worth your child's soul. If you can't control TV, for example, consider eliminating it altogether, or keep it in a closet and bring it out only for special occasions to watch as a family.

Remember that you are at war with the forces of evil.

Satan is out to get your children. He succeeds far too often.

Genesis 13:12,13 – Remember the story of Lot. For the sake of material gain, he chose to associate with evil people. Though he himself was grieved by the evil, he did not protect his family as he should have (2 Peter 2:7,8). In the end he lost, not only all those material possessions that he had desired, but also his wife, children, and sons-in-law to sin (Genesis 19).

The same is happening to many families today, and one of the main evils that causes many children to be lost is corrupt entertainment. We can overcome the problem. But we must realize we are at war and take adequate defensive measures!

Suppose you lived in the age before television, movies, and computers had been invented. You knew nothing about them, but someone came to your home and showed you a typical evening of modern TV or music or video games. What would you do? Throw it out! But today we often allow in our homes that which we really know to be immoral, because we have gradually come to accept it!

Growing a Godly Marriage

Peers

Parents need to have a plan, how to deal with this problem.

Here are some suggestions. (You may find other ways, but these are some suggestions that harmonize with Bible principles.)

* Get to know your children's friends. Have them visit in your home.

* Never let your children go anywhere, including dates, unless you know the people they will be with, where they are going, when they'll be back, etc.

Illustration: If a stranger asked to borrow your car, wouldn't you want to get to know the person first? Wouldn't you want assurance where they were going, what they would do, whom they would be with, and when they'd be back? Aren't your children more valuable than your car?

* Train your children, from a very early age, to choose the right kind of friends. Especially teach them the importance of marrying a Christian (and that dating leads to marriage).

* Give your children opportunities to associate with good young people. Arrange times for young people to be together. Don't expect the church to do it. You do it for your children's good.

* Train your children to talk about the gospel with their peers. It is not wrong to associate with people who are not Christians. Jesus did so, but He did it so He could have opportunity to teach. Children should learn to invite other children to Bible classes, discuss right and wrong, set up Bible studies, etc. If they date non-Christians, let them be these kinds of dates.

* Exercise your authority to determine who your child may or may not be friends with. Young people think, "My folks have no right to tell me who my friends will be." But God says, "Children obey your parents..." (Ephesians 6:1) and says parents must train up children to serve God. If parents determine some young person is a harmful influence on their child, they have every right to intervene, just the same as they can make any other decision for the good of their child.

There may be other ideas that help. But the parents are obligated to plan ways to deal with problems caused by peers.

Education

Parents must plan how to effectively deal with problems in education.

Here are some suggestions. Other choices may work, but parents are obligated to **deal with the issues**, not just throw up our hands and do nothing and hope the children turn out all right.

* Investigate what's happening. Visit the schools. Get to know your child's teachers and administrators. Read your child's textbooks.

Volunteer to work at school activities. Read books that inform you what problems to look for in the schools (check www.eagleforum.org). Investigate school activities **before** your child gets involved. Find out if a class or extra-curricular activity will involve missing services, immodesty, false teaching, etc.

* Make clear to all involved that your child will not participate in certain activities. Write out a list such areas of concern (sex education, evolution, abortion, homosexuality, etc.). Talk to your child's teacher about them. Have the list put in your child's school record and state in writing that your child is not to be presented any such material without your express prior approval.

* If a problem exists in a class or activity, talk to people in charge and work out an arrangement for your child to be excused or given some other activity, etc.

* Talk with children at home about matters of concern. Try to get open communication. (But don't rely entirely on this because sometimes children don't talk about their problems).

* Teach your children the truth diligently and regularly about the concerns they are facing in the schools. Have regular studies at home, etc.

* Limit your child's involvement in school activities. Schools increasingly dominate children's time. They get them younger and keep them longer. They promote day-care, preschool, kindergarten, after-school activities, and sometimes before-school activities. All this strengthens the school's influence and weakens the family's influence.

Instead of this, de-emphasize school involvement, and emphasize family and church activities. Have recreation and work together as a family. Worship God together, study His word, and pray, visit in homes of other Christian, attend all church assemblies and classes, visit area gospel meetings, clean the building, do personal work together, help them learn to teach class, etc.

* Stand for the truth regardless of the consequences. If it means your child's grades suffer or he faces ridicule or embarrassment, so be it. First-century Christians went to prison, were beaten and even died rather than participate in error. Parents must teach children to **sacrifice** and suffer for the cause of Christ.

* You may need to consider alternative forms of education: private school or home schooling. These may not work for everybody, but for many people they are a true blessing.

* Remember God gave **you** the responsibility to train your children to serve Him (Ephesians 6:4). And he will hold you accountable. **Even when your children are at school, you (not the school) have the ultimate responsibility** for seeing that your child is rightly trained. If the schools cooperate with your authority,

wonderful. If not, then it's your job to take whatever steps are needed for the good of your child.

Conclusion

Luke 6:46 – Why do you call Me "Lord, Lord," and do not do the things which I say? Authority is a critical issue facing society. Children must learn the proper attitude toward authority in their homes, as they relate to the authority of their parents. The way we exercise authority toward our children will very likely determine their eternal destiny.

Are the children in your home learning proper authority relationships?

Key #6: Motivation: Punishments and Rewards

Parents would prefer that their children simply obey them by their own choice. But in practice, this does not always happen. Often the child's will conflicts with that of the parent. Then, if the child is to learn respect for authority and do what we believe to be best for him, we must still get them to obey us. How can we lead a child to obey when he would rather not?

The answer is that ***parents must motivate the child to obey***. Whatever reasons the child has for not obeying, we must give him stronger reasons to obey! This is done by rewards and punishments. When the child obeys, we make him glad by giving him a pleasant experience. When he disobeys, we make him sorry by giving an unpleasant experience. He eventually learns it is to his advantage to obey.

Psychologists call this "reinforcement." It is used in training animals. Obedience leads to a pleasant result; disobedience leads to an unpleasant result. We are dealing, not with animals, but with children who have intelligence and emotional needs. Above all, they have a spirit in the image of God and will eventually receive an eternal destiny based on their conduct before God. This is why we already emphasized love and instruction. Nevertheless, the principles of rewards and punishments are useful and Scriptural.

Consider how these principles can be used in training children.

Growing a Godly Marriage

Spanking

Many child-rearing "authorities" oppose the use of spanking. Psychologist Linda Budd wrote that, if you spank your child, you should, "Apologize. Own up to your mistake" (via Greg Gwin, *Good News*, 5/28/95). So, consider a Biblical defense of spanking.

Spanking Is Taught in the Bible.

God's word commands parents to use spanking when needed.

Proverbs 22:15 – Foolishness is bound in a child's heart, but the rod drives it from him. Parents must exercise authority and give their children rules. But all children, at times, will test those limits. Then punishment is needed to "restrain" them.

Proverbs 19:18 – Chasten the son while there is still hope. This is for his good. Children must be taught obedience while they are young, even before their reasoning ability matures. If you wait till later, they may be past "hope." (See also Proverbs 29:15; 23:13; 20:30.)

Proverbs 13:24 – One who does not spank his son, when it is needed, hates his son. One who loves his son will chasten him. God says spanking is not an act of hatred. On the contrary, **properly done, spanking is an act of love, and those who deny the value of spanking are the ones who God says hate children.**

The issue of spanking boils down to the authority of God and the inspiration of the Bible. A psychologist may question my intelligence. But when he challenges spanking, he is disagreeing, not with me, but with God. And God is smarter than all the psychologists put together!

Spanking is compared to God's punishment of his people – Hebrews 12:5-11.

God Himself compares His chastisement of people to earthly fathers who chasten their sons. God says that all fathers will chasten their children; otherwise, it indicates that the child is illegitimate (verses 6-8)!

Further, this chastening is an act of love, not hatred (verse 6), because it results in good for the child (verses 10,11). Some claim that punishing children produces resentment and misunderstanding, causing them to hate and disrespect their parents. But God says that discipline leads the child to respect the father (verse 9).

If parents should not punish children, then it follows that God should not punish evil men. But He does punish evil men, and no one is wiser than He is. He is our perfect example of a good Father.

Finally, note that this is a New Testament Scripture. Some people question our use of Old Testament Scripture on this subject; but here is a New Testament Scripture that teaches the same thing. In fact, verses 5,6 quote Proverbs 3:11,12. God's teaching on this matter is the same today as it was in the Old Testament!

People who deny the value of spanking, therefore, are denying the wisdom and authority of God Himself. Some don't know this; others do it knowingly. But regardless, to oppose spanking is to directly attack the inspiration of the Bible and the infallibility of God. Parents must understand and appreciate the value of spanking, regardless of what any human "authorities" claim.

(Compare Revelation 3:19; Deuteronomy 8:5; 28:15; Exodus 7-12; 2 Thessalonians 1:8-10; etc.)

Spanking Works Where Other Methods Fail.

People who oppose spanking, offer no workable alternatives.

Some authorities say to "reason" with the child till he agrees.

"Intelligent parents rarely resort to corporal punishment ... An intelligent disciplinary method is the use of reasoning at the child's level of understanding..." – *Growing Superior Children*, pages 452 (via *Plain Truth about Child Rearing*, p. 26). My translation: "Spanking proves you lack intelligence. If you were smart enough, you could talk them into obeying!"

This statement flatly denies Bible teaching. Reasoning with children is important and should not be neglected, but it has limits. Often immediate obedience is needed, as when a child is playing in the street and a car is coming! Some children are too young and inexperienced to understand the wisdom of the parents' reasons. And often the child is just too stubborn and self-willed to listen. In such cases, no amount of reasoning will change him.

Dr. Dobson (DTD, pages 18ff) tells of a young mother who had been taught to reason her child into obedience. When she put her three-year-old son in his crib, he spat in her face. When she tried to reason with him, he repeated it. She finally fled the room as he spat on the back of the door! She said she could never control him after that; as a teenager he rebelled against every request she made.

We need to reason with our children as part of our instruction. But there are times when every child determines to have his own way, and no amount of reasoning will convince him. The result becomes a war of attrition, in which the child will continue arguing till he wears you down. He must be taught that "crime does not pay." Pain works wonders.

Again, some suggest that we just "control the child's environment."

We are told to not make demands and children won't rebel. Just remove all temptation and give the children recreation and interesting toys; then they will never want to do bad things. My translation: "Just let the kid have his own way, and there will be no conflicts."

Again, there is value in keeping temptation out of the child's way. But to do this to the exclusion of spanking contradicts the Bible, and experience shows that it simply does not work.

Matthew 16:24 – To be a follower of Jesus we must learn to deny and control ourselves. The child who is given everything he wants never learns self-sacrifice and self-denial. He becomes self-centered and thinks the world must always adapt to him and give him what he wants. As he grows up, his demands become bigger and bigger, till finally his parents cannot satisfy his demands. His environment cannot always be controlled, so sooner or later he must face temptation and learn to control himself. Otherwise, he is destined for major trouble in life, because he thinks the world owes him a living; but the world will not always give him what he wants. The result is unhappy, miserable delinquents, rebels, and criminals such as flood our land.

Dr. Dobson (DTD, pages 14,15) tells of another family where the parents always gave their daughter whatever she wanted, never crossed her, and never made demands. She became a selfish and disrespectful teenager, throwing terrible tantrums if she did not get her way. They tried to give a party to please her, but she brought in disrespectful, rebellious friends who proceeded to tear things up. When the mother said something that angered her, the daughter "struck her down and left her helpless" lying in a pool of blood on the floor. The daughter then went out unconcerned to dance with her friends in the backyard.

This is an extreme example. But the point is that without spanking and physical punishment child rearing is doomed to failure. Spanking uses relatively mild and temporary pain to teach the child lessons that will help him avoid much greater hardships and trouble later in life and in eternity. In this way, spanking benefits the child and is therefore an act of love.

Objections to Spanking Are Not Valid.

Some say spanking leads to child abuse or even constitutes child abuse.

The parenting text *Child Growth and Development,* page 315, says physical punishment is "unsatisfactory" because, "All physical punishment has the danger of turning into child abuse or causing injury when the adult is really angry. For this reason alone, it should be avoided."

Sweden outlawed spanking on the grounds that it is child abuse. In this country, schoolteachers are generally forbidden to spank, and some people have tried to pass laws forbidding parents to spank their own children. Often overly zealous social workers harass parents and call them into court, simply because parents exercise Scriptural discipline.

We do not deny that child abuse exists. We deplore it as much or more than others do. But we affirm that scriptural spanking, rather than constituting child abuse, actually helps prevent it.

We have shown by the Scriptures that exercise of Scriptural discipline is an expression of love for children. It is done for the child's well being. In contrast, the child abuser loses sight of the child's well-being and acts from selfishness and anger. Such conduct flatly contradicts the Bible and is not what we are defending.

Actually, proper spanking helps avoids child abuse. The reason people abuse children is that they do not know how to properly control them. The children's conduct frustrates and angers the parent till finally he loses control and, in a fit of anger and frustration, does lasting harm to the child. If instead parents would learn to discipline their children when the need first becomes evident, the matter would never get so out of hand.

Others say spanking makes the child feel guilty and destroys his self-esteem.

"The chief danger of punishment is that it makes the child feel guilty – that he is bad, naughty" – *Complete Book of Mothercraft*, page 391 (via *Plain Truth about Child Rearing*, page 21).

But wait! What if the child has been bad and naughty? What if he is guilty, but doesn't feel guilty? What if he has been disrespectful or has done what could lead him into sin? It sounds like punishment is just what he needs!

A fundamental error of modern psychology is that it often denies evil and guilt. It fails to hold people accountable for their misdeeds. It teaches them to have a high self-image by whitewashing and denying their guilt. But people remain unhappy and maladjusted, because subconsciously they still know something is wrong. Worse yet, this approach leaves people with no real solution for their problem. The truth often is they are guilty; but by leading them to deny guilt, psychology leaves them with no way to remedy it.

The Bible teaches us to recognize that, when people do wrong, they are guilty and should be told so. If they stubbornly refuse to admit guilt, they should be punished so they suffer for their wrong till they admit it. This is true of children and adults.

Proverbs 20:30 – Blows and stripes cleanse away guilt and reach the inner depths of the heart. Like many Bible principles, spanking is not just an external act. It reaches the heart and teaches the child to become an upright, righteous person. It molds godly character.

The Bible does not just teach about guilt; it also has a **solution** for the guilt. When one is sorry, repents, apologizes, and corrects his conduct, he receives forgiveness from God and from other people

(Matthew 6:12-15; Luke 17:3,4). One reason many people do not appreciate the value of spanking, is that they do not understand God's concept of guilt and forgiveness. Spanking has the major advantage of harmonizing with the Bible concept of guilt and forgiveness and instilling that concept in our children.

Others say spanking teaches children to use violence.

Sociology Professor Murray Strauss wrote: "Spanking teaches kids that when someone is doing something you don't like and they won't stop doing it, you hit them" (via Greg Gwin, *Good News*, 5/28/95). So supposedly, spanking teaches children that "might makes right," and if we are bigger and stronger than others we can get our way by violence.

That may sound reasonable, and that could happen if we are not motivated by proper concern for the child. But the truth is just the opposite when we discipline properly. An **un**disciplined child is the one who tends to use violence. He throws fits in rebellion against his parents' authority, but he never suffers for such conduct. As he gets older, he learns to throw bigger fits, including physical violence against those who don't let him have his way, just as in the examples we have mentioned. But if instead, when he is small, he is punished for his fits and is not allowed to get his way by such conduct, then he learns that violence does not pay.

Spanking, coupled with love and instruction, teaches children the vital principle that **only people in positions of proper authority have the right to punish others.** Parents do no spank just because they are bigger and can "get their own way" by violence. Rather, they have God-given authority to train a child for the child's good. Children have no right to punish others, because they do not have authority. Children can learn to see the difference.

Again, this teaches the child to respect other authority roles, such as God Himself, civil rulers, etc. (Romans 12:19; 13:1-7). Those who say that spanking teaches children to be violent are, perhaps unknowingly, denying the right of God, civil rulers, and all authority figures to require a penalty of those who flaunt authority. In short, they have a perverted concept of authority.

Others say spanking simply does not work.

"The best that can be said for spanking is that it sometimes clears the air. But it isn't worth the price, and it usually doesn't work" – *The Complete Book of Mothercraft*, page 367 (via *Plain Truth about Child Rearing*, p. 26.) Parents often make similar statements: "I tried spanking my child, but it just didn't make any difference."

Spanking can fail, but only when it has been misused. You are not guaranteed success just because you occasionally spank your child. Spanking must be administered properly (see notes below). And it must be used in connection with love, instruction, and rewards, as we discuss elsewhere.

And spanking must be used diligently and consistently. You cannot overcome months of improper training with just a few spankings. You will not succeed if you get discouraged and quit trying after a few attempts, nor if you occasionally spank a child for some offenses but then just ignore other times when he is naughty.

Proper training must also begin early. It is possible to wait till a child is so mature that his bad habits are thoroughly ingrained. You still should attempt to use right methods, but it may be too late to change his conduct (Proverbs 19:18).

Those who object to spanking fall into one or more of the following categories: (1) they are ignorant of the Bible, or (2) they simply reject the Bible teaching, or (3) they have observed parents who misuse the Biblical concept of discipline. In short, whenever people oppose spanking, at the root of their opposition lies a misunderstanding of authority.

But anything good can be misused; Satan consistently leads people to pervert what is good. Like fire, electricity, atomic energy, and other powerful forces, spanking can be misused and cause great damage. But the fact there are dangers in these areas does not keep us from using them for the good they can accomplish. When people understand God-given concepts of authority and practice them wisely, they will find that spanking is both useful and indispensable.

Rewards as a Form of Control

Some parents act as though controlling children is entirely a matter of punishment. They never give rewards and sometimes speak as though they think it is wrong to do so. One book I read calls it "bribery." So, consider a Biblical defense of using rewards in raising children.

Rewards Are Part of Life as a Principle of Authority.

Parents ought to prepare children to live in the "real world." But when they are on their own, it is right for them to expect rewards for their labor. Why should we not teach them this by rewarding them as they grow up?

Luke 10:7 – The laborer is worthy of his wage, but lazy, negligent workers do not deserve to be rewarded. (See also Matthew 25:14-30; 20:1-15; James 5:4; 1 Corinthians 9:6-14; 1 Timothy 5:17,18; Ephesians 4:28; 2 Thessalonians 3:10).

Men do not work on a job simply for the fun of it. We rightly expect to be paid, and we hope that the people who benefit from our labors will express appreciation.

1 Peter 2:13,14 – Rulers should praise citizens who do good, not just punish criminals. This carries over into other areas of life. Children who work hard on schoolwork, get a better grade. When people are overweight, if they exercise they may be rewarded by losing weight.

Proverbs 27:2 – Let another man praise you and not your own lips. Children who are not praised may grow up bragging and showing off to get attention. When parents give proper praise, their children learn not to brag on themselves.

So one reason for rewarding children is to prepare them for life!

God Rewards People for Their Service.

Hebrews 11:6 – God is a rewarder of those who diligently seek Him. He often rewarded Israel for their faithfulness (Deuteronomy 28:1,2ff). The New Testament promises that those who are faithful will receive all spiritual blessings in this life (Ephesians 1:3) and eternal life at the Judgment (Romans 8:14,17; 2:6-11).

God does not just punish evil; He also rewards good. This has always been a fundamental part of the Divine nature. If Hebrews 12 uses the fact that God chastises us as proof we should chastise our children, then shouldn't we also imitate His example of rewarding good? Remember that God is our perfect example of a father.

By using rewards as well as punishments, we help children understand the true nature of their Heavenly Father, and we teach them how to properly relate to authority.

A Bible Example of Parental Rewards

Luke 15:20-24 – When the prodigal son repented and returned from sin, the father kissed him, rejoiced, and gave a feast in his honor. He rewarded the son for doing what was right!

One way to reward a child is by letting him work for physical things he wants: money or some item he wants. But this does not mean the child should be paid for everything he does. His parents are already providing him with food, clothes, shelter, etc. If the laborer is worthy of his reward, then the child already owes it to the parents to work in return for all that the parents do for the child! And especially in spiritual matters, children need to learn the value of deferring their reward till judgment day, not necessarily expecting immediate rewards for serving God.

Romans 13:7 – Give honor to whom honor is due. Another form of reward parents ought to emphasize is expressing appreciation and giving praise. This is simply a matter of showing gratitude. (Matthew 25:21)

The nature of the rewards should be a matter of the parents' good judgment. Use your ingenuity. Learn to watch for things your children want. When they ask, "May I do this or go there or have that ...," try responding, "If you'll do this work first, then you may." You may promise to read a book to the child after he picks up his toys. As children grow older, perhaps you can pay an allowance for special jobs he does.

The point is to give pleasant results to reward the child for doing good as well as giving unpleasant consequences for failing to do good. This is both Biblical and practical: it works.

Other Useful Methods of Control

I cannot give a complete list of good methods parents can use to motivate children, but I can suggest some possibilities as illustrations. Parents should use their ingenuity.

Acceptable Substitutes

If a child has been corrected for some wrong or has been forbidden to do something unacceptable, you may offer him an acceptable alternative rather than leave him disappointed or tempted to disobey your instructions.

If he cannot ride his tricycle because it is raining, suggest some inside game or activity.

If you teach him not to go to the prom, offer him a night out with the family or a banquet with other Christian friends.

This too is Biblical. God does not just forbid sin; He tells us the good we should replace it with (Ephesians 4:22-32). This approach leaves the child with much less temptation to do wrong, and teaches him to have a positive outlook and be content even when he cannot get his way.

But don't go too far. Don't use this as an excuse to avoid punishing rebellion. When a child is rebelling, he should first be punished, not rewarded by giving him something pleasant to do.

Withholding Privileges

Rewards are given only to those who deserve them. When a child misbehaves, withholding a privilege or reward may be an appropriate punishment. Usually such punishments are most effective if the connection between the punishment and the crime is fairly obvious.

If he doesn't finish a job or homework, he can't go play till he is finished.

If he disobeys rules about some toy, the toy is put up for a while where he can't play with it.

If he misbehaves with his friends, then he cannot visit with them for a period of time.

If he does not come home on time, he is "grounded" and can't go where he wants for a while.

If an older teen uses the car irresponsibly, his use of the car is withdrawn for a while.

Apology

Matthew 5:23,24; Luke 17:3,4 – The Bible teaches us to apologize to people we have wronged. Parents should require children to practice this principle. When the child wrongs another child, an adult, or the parents themselves, the child must apologize.

This also constitutes good discipline, because it is hard to admit our error face-to-face to the person we wronged. The child is not likely to soon repeat the act that led to this consequence.

Natural Consequences

Some acts naturally lead to unpleasant consequences that teach the child a lesson without the parents' having to punish them.

Luke 15:14-17 – The Prodigal Son's father allowed his son to suffer the consequences of doing wrong. The boy reached the bottom, but nobody bailed him out (including his father). As a result, he "came to himself" and repented. Modern parents should learn the lesson. (Compare 1 Samuel 8:9ff.)

Sometimes this method is the only one children will listen to. They may have to learn some lessons the hard way. If they refuse to listen to us, don't protect them from the consequences of their wrong.

If a child torments a cat, warn him to quit. If he continues, the cat may scratch him.

If a child makes a foolish debt, make him work to pay it off.

If he misbehaves at school, don't take his part against the teacher or school authorities. Let them punish him.

If he misbehaves toward a neighbor (as by damaging their property), make him go face the angry neighbor and fix what he broke.

If he breaks a law and the judge fines him, make him work to pay off the fine.

If the consequences are too severe, we may prefer a lesser punishment (spank the child instead of letting him burn himself on a hot stove). But sometimes a child simply won't learn from the parents' teaching.

When children live in sin, they often want their parents to accept and support them despite the sin. Instead, parents should insist that either the sin stops or the support stops.

Many parents "bail out" their children when they get in trouble, so the children never learn responsibility. Sometimes the best punishment is to let the child suffer for his error and don't protect him from the consequences.

Logical Consequences

Sometimes we can think of a punishment that is logically associated with the wrong deed. It "fits the crime."

When a child accidentally spills or breaks something, spanking usually is not appropriate. Instead, have him clean up what he spilled or pay to replace what he broke.

If he misbehaves in how he uses a toy or equipment (bicycle), put the toy away where he can't use it for a specified time.

If he mistreats other family members, isolate him from the family as by sitting in the corner.

If children squabble and can't get along, they may be separated from one another so they can't play together.

Divine Corrections for Sin

When the child's conduct is sinful, we should use the same methods for correction that we should with others who sin. This includes:

Use God's word to instruct and rebuke them.

2 Timothy 3:16,17 (4:2-4) – Use the Bible to show them where they are wrong and warn them of the consequences. The Scriptures are "profitable for reproof."

Make clear that you are acting for the child's good. Don't lead them to think the Bible is a tool for parents to get their own way. Show them that this is God's will and they must obey God.

Cooperate with other Christians and the church, when they rebuke the child.

Galatians 6:1 – If Christians talk to our child about his sins, the parents may become defensive and protective. Instead, we should realize that this is for our child's good. We should appreciate people who care enough to help. Remember the father of the prodigal, who allowed his son to suffer the consequences of his sin till the son repented.

2 Thessalonians 3:6,14,15 – If the church exercises Scriptural discipline because our child sinned, we should cooperate and respect the church's decision. The Old Law taught parents to actively participate in congregational punishment of erring children (Deuteronomy 21:18-21; 13:6-11; Zechariah 13:3). If we oppose Scriptural discipline, we become a partaker of the sin – 2 John 10,11.

Pray for the child to do right.

James 5:16 – Confess your faults to one another and pray for one another. When the child admits his error, pray to God to help him do right. If he is old enough to be a Christian, then his disobedience to you was also a sin against God. Have him confess to God and pray for forgiveness. (Acts 8:22; Matthew 6:12; 21:28-32; 2 Corinthians 7:10; 1 John 1:8-10; Proverbs 28:13)

Parents may find other means of motivating children. But the principle always is: give pleasant consequences for good behavior, unpleasant consequences for bad behavior.

Guidelines for Proper Use of Punishments and Rewards

To be effective and Scriptural, punishments and rewards must be administered according to certain rules. The mere fact you use spanking (or other punishments) and rewards, does not of itself guarantee parental success.

Never Inflict Lasting Damage to a Child.

Remember that you seek to punish for the child's **good,** not for his harm. We seek only temporary pain to change the child's conduct. To inflict lasting harm is unloving, does not accomplish the purpose of punishment, and violates the command not to discourage our children (Ephesians 6:4; Colossians 3:21).

Yet many parents do harm their children. Child abuse is a definite problem in our society. Literally thousands of children every year are beaten to death by their parents, left abandoned, or otherwise inflicted with lasting harm. All such conduct neglects parental responsibility and violates Scripture.

Motivate Children by Prompt Actions, Not by Arguing and Yelling.

Some parents try to control children by yelling or endless talk.

Dr. Dobson gives this example:

I knew of a family with four of the world's most undisciplined children. These youngsters were the terrors of their neighborhood; they were disrespectful, loud, and aggressive. They roamed in and out of garages, helping themselves to tools and equipment. It became necessary for neighbors to remove handles from outside water faucets, because these children enjoyed leaving the water running when the families were gone. It was interesting to observe the method of discipline used by their mother, because whatever it was, it didn't work. Her system of controlling children boiled down to a simple formula: she would rush out the front door about once every hour, and scream: "I have had it with you; I have had it with you children!" Then she would turn and go back into the house. The children never even looked up at her. If they knew she was there they gave no indication of it. She apparently felt it was sufficient for her to come out like a cuckoo clock and remind them that she was still on the job – DTD, pages 9,10.

We may know such methods are ineffective, yet may make the same mistake in other ways. We may nag and harp, threaten and scold: "What's the matter with you, Son. You never do what I say. What am I going to do with you? It seems like you're always getting into something. Why can't you do what you're told? Other children obey their parents, why can't you? Etc., etc., etc." "This is the last time I'm going to tell you that this is the last time I'm going to tell you!"

In church meetings a child misbehaves, so parents repeatedly whisper to them, tug at them, shake them, grab them, and sit them down. But the problem continues.

Others try to control children by getting loud or by long lectures. This was commonly one of our mistakes. I yelled. Karen gave long lectures. This may not be sinful, but it is not effective.

The child simply gets used to the noise and turns it off. It may work at first, but then he learns to gauge how loud, how angry, how long you threaten and scold before you do anything. Then he pushes you to the limit. He pays no attention until you reach the fever pitch where he thinks you are about to take action.

Further, the parent's verbal barrage often results in a return barrage. We scold; he argues and fusses. We scold louder and longer; he argues and fusses louder and longer. Other family members overhear. The result is that everyone becomes angry, frustrated, and upset. And the parent finally ends up having to punish the child anyway, so what was the advantage?

Do not argue or yell. Use words to instruct or rebuke, but use actions to punish.

Proverbs 13:24 – He who spares his rod hates his son, but he who loves him disciplines him ***promptly*** (NKJV – the footnote says "early"; compare Hebrews 12:5-11). We think we are showing love for the child by postponing punishment, but we would show more love and have a better relationship if we would just punish and get it over with.

Here is something I learned from how some of our children deal with our grandchildren:

1) They make sure the child understands what they expect. They say, "Look at me," or "Come here and look at me." The child must stop playing, etc., and listen to the parents' instructions.

2) Then they say, "Do you understand." The child must respond, "Yes, sir" (or "Yes, Mother," etc.). This avoids the excuse, "I didn't hear you," or "I didn't understand you."

3) Then if the child proceeds to disobey, apparently he does not *want* to obey. So, it is time to punish with *actions*. (This is a better approach than what I often used.)

If you learn to discipline "promptly," soon you won't have to argue with a child. He will obey "promptly," because he now knows that you will back up your words with action.

Arguing and yelling beget arguing and yelling; action begets action.

Always Control Yourself When Disciplining.

Ephesians 4:26 – Be angry and do not sin. Anger toward children is not necessarily sinful. But when we become angry and agitated, there is danger that we may make bad decisions. We may lose control and cause serious harm. So, we really should control ourselves, and administer discipline calmly. But how do we accomplish this?

Interestingly enough, the answer is the same as the last point: *Take action early, before the situation gets out of hand.* Obtain action from the child by taking action yourself. He is not likely to do what you say until he thinks you will take action. So don't postpone the action. When the child does something that you will eventually punish him for if he does not change, warn him calmly, making sure he understands. If he still does not obey, calmly punish him.

Consistent application of this approach leads to less arguing, less anger, less upset, and less threatening. But the result will also be *less punishment*, in the long run. Why? Because when the child learns that you mean what you say, he will act when you tell him to, instead of agitating till you have to punish him. *By punishing more promptly, you end up punishing less frequently.* Greater commitment to action leads to decreased need for action. More is less.

Yes, you can and should learn to punish children calmly. Remember it: Arguing begets arguing; action begets action.

Measure Your Effectiveness by the Child's Obedience.

Ephesians 6:1 – Children *obey* your parents. Obedience is the goal of our training!

Don't judge effectiveness by how much the child cries or what the child says.

Some parents spank hard enough to cause crying, but not hard enough to cause obedience! They give little smacks that hurt very little. The child fusses so the parent stops punishing. And the child continues to do as he wants.

Once after my mother had spanked me, I told my sister, "It didn't hurt. I just cried so she'd quit." My sister told Mother, and Mother did the job again to make sure it hurt!

The fact a child cries does not prove he is really sorry enough to obey. Some crying really expresses rebellion, protest, or anger. Children may hope their crying will get on their parents' nerves, make them feel guilty, or embarrass them if others hear it. Or maybe the parents will just get tired of all the fuss and trouble, and decide to drop the matter. ***But if the child isn't doing what you told him to do, your job isn't done yet, no matter how much he cries. Punish him some more till he obeys you!***

Matthew 21:28-31 – A son said he would obey his father's and work in the vineyard, but he did not go. Some children ***say*** they will obey, but then don't. Some are sweetly pleasant and say the right things, but they don't follow through to obey. This is just another form of rebellion.

Determine the methods you use by what WORKS.

Do not automatically resort to spanking. Maybe with a certain child in a certain situation, just a good discussion will solve the matter. Or maybe you can give a lesser punishment or take away a privilege. Different children react differently to different approaches. Learn what works best with each child under various circumstances. ***But use what produces obedience.***

Be sure your rewards are really something the child likes, and your punishments are something he dislikes. In the Uncle Remus' tales, Br'er Fox caught Br'er Rabbit and wanted to punish him. Br'er Rabbit convinced Br'er Fox that he would suffer terribly if Br'er Fox would fling him into the briar patch. But when it happened, Br'er Rabbit was happy as could be, because the briar patch was his home!

Some punishments are simply inadequate. Some parents spank on a diaper or on an older child's blue jeans. It makes a loud noise, but the child feels very little. I always pulled my children's clothing up or down and spanked on their bare thigh. It's a punishment. Make it hurt!

You may think you punished the child enough. Or he may ***say*** he will obey. But if he doesn't change his behavior, then apparently he doesn't consider the punishment to be severe enough.

Continue working on the problem till the child acts as he should.

Never let the child win a battle of wills. With many children there will come a time – perhaps several or many times – when he stubbornly sets his will against yours and dares you to make him obey. The Bible calls it "stiff-necked." When that happens, you must not lose that battle.

If you must spank the child a dozen times, he must learn that, when you "put your foot down," then he is not going to win. The point is not that the parent is just stubborn or egotistical. It is a principle of authority for everyone's good.

If the child finds out that he can get his way by being stubborn enough long enough, then he will be ten times more stubborn next time. But if you can prove without question, while the child is a preschooler, that what you say is the way it will be, then he will challenge your authority far less frequently in later years, including the rebellious teen years.

This is not to say we should refuse to listen to reason. If the child can give good reasons for us to change our minds, that is one matter. But we are discussing a conflict of wills in which the child just doesn't want to do what we told him to do. In that case, you must keep on punishing until the child submits. You must not let him have his way! The goal is **obedience**.

Consider the Reasons Why Your Child Acts as He Does.

How you respond to a child should be determined by why he acts as he does.

Ephesians 6:4 – Do not provoke children to anger.

Perhaps a child is simply not able to understand or do what you asked. Maybe you did not explain your instructions clearly enough. Maybe he honestly forgot due to time lapse, tiredness, excitement, etc. Maybe he acts as he does because of an unfilled emotional need: fear, insecurity, or a desire for love and attention. These situations should be handled differently from outright rebellion.

But when the child knows (or ought to know) what you want but is just rebellious, self-willed, stubborn, and does not want to do what you want, this child must be punished.

How can we determine the child's motives?

This is not always easy. It requires thought, experience, and knowledge of the child. Parents should discuss these matters together. Here are some thoughts to help.

Put yourself in the child's place. When you were his age, how would you have acted or felt? What treatment would have led you to obey? "Do unto others..." (Matthew 7:12).

Consider how the child would act if he WANTED to do what you tell him to do.

Suppose you tell Johnny to do something, but he fusses and squirms and cries. You may think he is too tired or maybe he's sick. But five minutes later, he is doing something he likes, so now he is all smiles and happiness. That proves little Johnny can be pleasant if he *wants* to – it's your job to see to it that he wants to!

Maybe Johnny says he is too sick to go to school, then he wants to play with his toys or go outside and play. When I said I was too sick to go to school, my mother made me stay in bed all day to get better. Even school was better than that!

So, consider whether he is capable of understanding, remembering, and accomplishing the thing you asked of him if he really wanted to. If the answer is "yes," then your job is to give him sufficient reason to want to!

Generally, Children Should Be Disciplined in Private.

Sometimes a child misbehaves in public, in someone else's home, or in the presence of company. Disciplining him may be embarrassing, and in today's society could get you in trouble. But if you don't discipline him, he soon learns he can get away with misbehaving around others.

One solution is to call the child to you and inform him as privately as possible what you want (whisper, etc.). If firmer measures are needed, find or ask for a private place (restroom, bedroom, car, etc.). Take the child there and proceed to discipline. If he is old enough to understand, you may tell him you will discipline him when you get home.

When a child is noisy or disruptive during a church meeting, some parents don't want to take him out because they think it will disturb others. But not disciplining the child will only make matters worse, because the child will continue to disrupt other people.

When your child is distracting other people in worship assemblies, take him out and solve his problem. Then bring him back when he is under control so he will not distract others.

Never Offer a Child a Reward to Stop Misbehaving.

If he is already doing wrong, so you offer a reward to quit, then you have really rewarded and reinforced his misbehavior. Next time he wants a reward, he will misbehave hoping to receive the reward again.

Suppose you call Billy to come and he says, "No, I won't!" So, you offer him candy if he'll come. What will happen next time you call him? He'll remember that, if he says "No," he may get some candy!

The time to offer a reward is before the child has done anything wrong, while you are asking him to do something good. Or just give him the reward after he did the good deed, but don't wait till he's already doing something wrong and then offer him a reward to quit.

Talk to the Child Before and After You Punish Him.

Discuss the incident. Tell the child what he did wrong and what he should have done. After the punishment, make sure he is sorry: make him say he's sorry and make him promise to do right next time. If he refused to do something you told him to do, **take him back and make him do it**. Then be sure to tell the child you love him and you expect him to do better next time, etc. There are many advantages to this.

(1) It helps you keep calm.

(2) It makes sure the child knows why he was punished and what you expect in the future.

(3) It helps him remember the lesson. You certainly have his attention, so it is an excellent time to instruct him.

(4) It enables you to assure him of your love. Make sure he understands that you care about him, but you must not allow that kind of conduct.

(5) Often the child will feel bad just because he knows he disappointed you.

Gwendolyn Webb says to "make spanking an event" (TUAC, pages 168ff). She means don't just keep scolding and smacking a child, dragging out a situation. Take him out, talk to him, give him a real spanking, etc. Make it an event he will remember, so he is not likely to repeat the error.

Conclusion

Romans 11:22 – Therefore consider the goodness and severity of God: on those who fell, severity; but toward you, goodness, if you continue in His goodness.

God is a God of both rewards and punishments. He is our example of a good father. We should consider the principles He uses to motivate obedience and apply those principles in our homes according to the Scriptures.

Key #7: Consistency

Consistency is defined as "steadfast adherence to the same principles."

We have studied six "key" principles we must follow in order to raise godly children. But it is not enough to just **understand** these principles. We must **consistently** apply them – we must "steadfastly adhere" to them and continually apply the "same principles" without variation. This applies to all six areas we have already discussed:

(1) We must consistently remember that our **purpose** to raise our children to serve God.

(2) We must consistently **plan** our actions in harmony with God's word.

(3) We must consistently act in **love** making decisions according to what is best for the whole family.

(4) We must consistently **instruct** our children to know God's will.

(5) We must use **authority** consistently, expecting obedience and respect from children.

(6) We must consistently **motivate** children by diligent use of punishments and rewards.

Consistency of itself is not enough. It is possible to be consistently **wrong**! First we must learn the **right principles**, then we must steadfastly adhere to them.

Lack of consistency is one of the biggest problems facing parents. We often fail, not because we do not know what to do, but because we fail to diligently apply what we know.

Note some specific areas in which consistency is needed but is often lacking.

Consistency Between Parents

Both parents must "steadfastly adhere to the same principles." They must work together, not against one another.

Some Parents Disagree about Raising Children.

They may disagree about what rules to enforce or what punishments to give. They may even argue in front of a child.

Typically, one parent is strict and the other is lenient. One thinks the child is treated too harshly, so he/she compensates by being lenient to make up for the other parent's strictness. Then the other parent reacts by being even stricter to make up for their spouse's leniency. The result is a vicious circle in which the parents pull further and further apart.

Meanwhile, the child is completely confused. One parent punishes him, while the other one protects him. He doesn't know what the rules are. He has no security, but becomes a pawn in the parents' power struggle. But he soon learns to play the parents against one another. He goes to the parent who will let him have his way and uses that one to protect him from the other parent.

But the end result is the child does not really respect **either** parent. If they cannot decide the rules, why should he listen to them? Often great strife results within the family. And most tragically, the child never learns the qualities of character that either parent wants him to learn.

The Bible Deals with This Problem.

A Bible example: Isaac and Rebekah (Genesis 27)

Isaac determined to bless Esau, but Rebekah wanted the blessing to go to Jacob. Rebekah and Jacob deceived Isaac into blessing Jacob. The result was strife between Jacob and Esau so severe that Esau determined to kill Jacob, and Jacob had to flee from home.

Other passages

1 Corinthians 14:33 – God is not the author of confusion, but of peace. Such conflict between parents will surely lead to strife, not peace. God is not the cause of it and does not approve it.

Matthew 12:25 – A house divided against itself shall not stand. But a house is surely divided when parents disagree so about raising the children. They cannot possibly achieve their goal of raising godly children.

Ephesians 6:4 – Parents should not provoke children to wrath. But such inconsistency between the parents invariably causes wrath and discouragement on the part of the child.

The Bible Solution

Communicate.

Go back to step #2 – **planning**. Discuss the matter between yourselves based on the principles of God's word.

Even before marriage, you should discuss your basic approach to child raising. If one of you is fundamentally more lenient than the other or if there are other fundamental disagreements, discuss and reach understandings. Otherwise, marry someone else.

As you raise the children, continually discuss the principles you will follow. Try to decide the rules you will follow even **before** the problem comes up. Then there will be no need to argue at the time of the problem.

Communicate with your companion about specific situations, so the children cannot play you one against the other. If you give a rule to the children, tell your spouse about it so he/she will know. If a child asks your permission, ask, "What did your mother (or father) say?"

If you have a disagreement, don't argue in front of the child. Go elsewhere to talk about it.

Follow the Bible plan for authority in the home.

Ephesians 5:22-25 – The husband is head of the family, but he must act in love according to what is best for the family. Let the parents discuss the matter. Let the wife express her view respectfully. If appropriate, let the children express their views. Then let the father decide.

When the decision is made, the whole family should accept and honor it unless it requires the wife or children to do something sinful (Acts 5:29). No nagging, grumbling, or pouting. Specifically, the wife should submit to the husband's decision with the same good will that she wants the children to submit to her authority.

Consistency Between Words and Deeds

Parents should adhere steadfastly to the same principles in what we **do** compared to what we **say**. This is especially important in exercising authority.

Some Parents Do Not Keep Their Promises or Threats.

We tell our children they must do certain things; but if they stall or manipulate or flat out rebel, we don't make them do it. We may promise to give a punishment or reward, then we don't keep our word.

"If you don't ..., I'm going to ..." (or "If you will ..., then I will..."). But we don't do what we said.

Some parents make ridiculous threats that everyone knows they don't intend to carry out (and if they did carry it out, it would be sinful). "If you don't do what I say, I'll break every bone in your body." Such threats may be intended humorously, but often the parent appears to be quite serious and hopes the threat will lead the child to obey.

Such statements are often made by parents who try to control children by threats and anger, instead of by action (consider our earlier discussion about "Motivation"). If an act would be sinful to do, then what right do we have threatening to do it? Further, is it right to make threats or promises that we do not keep and in many cases have no intention of keeping?

Bible Principles Involved

Hebrews 10:23 – God is a perfect Father, and He is faithful to His promises. The fact that we know He will always keep His word helps motivate us to obey Him. If we could not trust Him to keep His promises, we would have little respect for Him and little reason to obey Him. Parents should likewise be faithful to their promises.

Romans 1:31 – Listed among those worthy of death are "covenant-breakers" (NKJV – "untrustworthy"). When we make promises we don't mean or we give our word but don't keep it, we are covenant-breakers or untrustworthy. Note that this is true whether we promise to give a reward or a punishment.

James 5:12 – Let your yes be yes and your no, no. Do not lightly say you will do a thing. If you don't mean it, don't say it. If you say you'll do it, then do it. This is true of both your "yes" and your "no."

If we promised a reward, we may think we are obligated to keep that promise, but it's OK to forget the promises of punishment. After all, the children don't want us to keep that kind of promise! But a promise is a promise, whether we promise a reward or a punishment. Failure to keep our promises is failure to be true to our word, and leads our children to disrespect us.

Colossians 3:21 – Do not provoke your children, lest they become discouraged. One way parents commonly provoke their children and discourage them is by failing to keep their word. One time we keep a threat or promise, but the next time we do not keep our word. How can children know whether or not to trust us?

Sometimes we may promise something, then later we realize it was a bad decision and it would be best for everyone if we change our mind. In that case, let us apologize for our mistake and explain our reason for changing. But don't lightly make threats or promises and do not lightly break them.

Consistency Between Children

Parents should not play favorites with their children, but should "steadfastly adhere to the same principles" regardless of the child.

Some Parents Are Partial to a Particular Child.

Parents may just like one child better than others or may play favorites for other reasons. They may be more lenient with one child. The favorite can do what is forbidden to others, or he is not punished as severely as another child would be for the same violation. He may receive gifts or favors that the others do not, etc.

Note that this does not mean we should ignore the fact that children have different circumstances. Sometimes children unfairly accuse parents of favoritism simply because one child is allowed to do what other children are not allowed to do, etc. But sometimes this is justified.

For example, an older child may be permitted to stay up later or go places when younger ones may not. The point is that rules should be the same for all children in the same circumstances. Rules should not be different just because we like one child better than another.

Favoritism harms all the children. The ones who are discriminated against may become jealous of the favorite, angry at the parents, and generally rebellious. They feel unloved and may deliberately disobey parents to get attention.

But the favorite is also hurt because he grows up thinking he deserves special treatment. He thinks he is more important than others, and can get away with breaking the rules. He will have great difficulty adjusting to real life, because the world won't treat him that way. And God certainly won't treat him that way.

Bible Principles Show the Dangers of Favoritism.

Remember that Isaac and Rebekah each had favorite children. Isaac loved Esau but Rebekah loved Jacob (Genesis 25:28). This resulted in so much strife that Esau sought to kill Jacob, and Jacob had to leave home.

Genesis 37:3,4 – Later Jacob also played favorites. His favorite son was Joseph, to whom he gave a coat of many colors. So much hatred resulted between his sons that the other brothers sold Joseph as a slave and almost killed him.

Acts 10:34,35; Romans 2:11 – God, who is a perfect father, does not play favorites. He does not respect persons, but treats us entirely according to how we act. Especially in administering rewards and punishments, God treats us on the basis of our conduct with no partiality.

James 2:1,8,9 – Likewise, God forbids us to show respect of persons. Partiality violates the Royal Law, which requires us to love our neighbor. Partiality is sinful just as surely as murder or adultery, yet many people are guilty right in their own homes!

Colossians 3:21 – Again, we must not provoke our children to discouragement. But one of the surest ways to discourage them is to treat them unjustly and unfairly. And one of the surest ways to be unjust is by practicing favoritism.

(Matthew 7:12)

Consistency Between Circumstances

We must "steadfastly adhere to the same principles" in the same circumstances *every time*. We must not allow today what we disallowed in the past under the same circumstances.

Sometimes Parent's Rules and Enforcement Are Not Reliable.

We may let our own mood, rather than the child's conduct, determine what rules or discipline we give. If we feel bad or had a bad day, we punish them for little things. But the next day we're in a better mood, so they avoid punishment when they do the same things.

Sometimes parents are too busy with other things and just don't pay attention to their children. We give them instructions; but then we get involved in work or conversation or watching TV so we overlook their disobedience. If we notice them, we correct them. But sometimes we just don't check up on them diligently.

Soon the child learns that, whether or not he gets punished, depends, not just on what he does, but also on the parents' mood or involvement in other things. So, it becomes a calculated risk on his part whether or not he can get away with disobedience. Or he becomes an amateur psychologist and tries to judge our moods. But what we have taught him is, not respect for authority, but manipulation of it.

Bible Principles

Hebrews 6:10 – God is not unjust. Jesus is not divided against Himself (1 Corinthians 1:13). How does God deal with our disobedience? Does the punishment we get depend on His mood? Does He get so involved in other things that He overlooks sin? God is the perfect example of consistency in dealing with our wrongs.

Matthew 23:23 – Justice is one of the weightier matters of the law. When rules are not enforced consistently, that is injustice. We would object if the civil government or an employer treated us that way. Let us practice justice by enforcing rules fairly in our families.

Colossians 3:21 – Again, we must not provoke our children to discouragement. Inconsistent enforcement of rules is one of the greatest causes of wrath and discouragement in children. Today the child is punished severely for doing the same kind of thing that he did yesterday with little or no punishment. This is unfair, and the child knows it.

Obviously, humans are limited in our ability to know every wrong each child does. Whereas God has perfect knowledge, at the best we are capable of being fooled. Children know this and do not disrespect us simply because occasionally things happen that we cannot know.

But the problem often occurs simply because we are not **trying** hard enough. We are too concerned for our own moods and our own interests, so we are not concerned enough about the conduct and training of our children. As a result, they get away with deliberate disobedience, because we are not "on the ball." That is injustice.

Consistency is the key that ties together all the other keys. We need consistency in applying all the principles we have studied – "steadfast adherence to the same principles."

Conclusion

If we practice these "key" principles we have studied, we will find that each of them in turn will instill a related quality in our children.

(1) If raising our children to serve God is our main **goal**, then the children will develop serving God as their main goal.

(2) If we **plan** our training of the children based on God's word, then our children will learn to plan their lives based on God's word.

(3) If we always act in **love** for our children, then they will learn to act in love for those around them.

(4) If we diligently **instruct** our children in God's word, they will develop, not only an understanding of God's word, but also an appreciation that they need to instruct their children.

(5) If we exercise proper **authority** toward our children, they will develop respect for authority and an understanding of how to exercise authority when they need to do so.

(6) If we **motivate** them by proper use of punishments and rewards, then they will learn to seek the rewards and avoid the punishments offered by God (and other authority figures).

(7) If we are **consistent** in applying these principles in training our children, then they will learn to do right consistently. Because we demand right conduct all the time, not just part of the time, they will learn to act right all the time.

The time will come when we must let our children be adults.

Our goal is not to keep them as children but to raise them to become godly adults. As they mature, we must let them accept the responsibility for guiding their lives without our control.

Genesis 2:24; Ephesians 5:22-25 – When they marry they leave our family; the husband becomes head of a new family. But even if they never marry, we must set them free to make their own choices. Paul and Jesus never married. Were they always subject to their parents?

When does this time come? The Bible does not define it in terms of age. Like the age of accountability, it is determined, not by age, but by maturity and ability to make mature choices.

The point is that, as our children grow, we must gradually give them increasing authority for their own lives. When we have protected and trained them so long, we will be tempted to want to keep them as children. But eventually they will leave our house and our authority. And we must be mature enough to let them go.

1 Timothy 5:4,16 – Finally, far sooner than we ever anticipated, the time will come when we will become dependent on them and they will be responsible to take care of us.

Parents are raising children, not just for life, but for eternity.

You and I will largely determine how our children live their lives and where they will be in eternity. Yet, many parents face this responsibility with far too little concern and far too little understanding of proper principles. We emphasize again that our goal as parents must be to **raise godly children**. While many people do not know how to do this, there is no need for us to be ignorant. God's word tells us the principles we should follow. To successfully raise godly children, we must understand and practice God's keys for raising children.

Sources Used

Dare to Discipline, Dr. James Dobson (abbreviated DTD).

Index of Leading Cultural Indicators, William Bennett, Heritage Foundation, et. al.; 1993 (abbreviated Bennett).

Training Up a Child, Gwendolyn Webb; The Old Landmarks, Denver CO, 1977 (abbreviated TUAC).

The Challenge of Fatherhood

Introduction:

Courageous **is the name of a movie and book by Randy Alcorn about five fathers.**

The sheriff challenges the men with a study: "The study shows when a father is absent, kids are five times more likely to commit suicide, ten times more likely to abuse drugs, fourteen times more likely to commit rape, and twenty times more likely to go to prison." (page 16)

The men eventually made a pledge to become the kind of fathers that God's word says fathers should be. The story tells the challenges and difficulties each of them faced.

The story has mild issues I do not endorse [modesty, dancing, denominational doctrines]. Nevertheless, with discernment, the movie or book will give important challenges to all of us.

Our purpose in this study is to consider important challenges facing fathers.

Modern philosophies and entertainment bombard us with perverted concepts of fathers. As a result, many men are confused about their role as a father. Worse yet, when the Bible speaks of God as our "Father," people who had a poor relationship with their earthly father often find it difficult to relate properly to their heavenly Father.

Consider the following challenging thoughts for fathers suggested by the movie/book:

The Challenge to Maintain Close
Family Ties

Consider the Problem of Absent Fathers

From National Fatherhood Initiative and Focus on the Family:

According to the US Census Bureau, 24 million children live without their biological father: that's one out of every three children. For teens aged 15-17, 54 percent of them their biological parents are no longer married or never did marry. Consider the consequences:

Poverty: The poverty rate for children with absent fathers is four times as great as children of married couples.

Unwed mothers: When fathers are absent, teenage daughters are seven times more like to become pregnant.

Drug and alcohol abuse: The National Center for Fathering says that fatherless children are 10 times more likely to abuse chemical substances.

Education: Fatherless children are twice as likely to drop out of high school.

Emotional problems, abuse, and crime: When fathers are absent, children are more likely to be abused, have behavioral problems, commit crime, and/or go to prison.

Doug Mainwaring left his wife and children to live as a gay man. Later, he returned to his family, primarily because he realized his children needed a mother and a father. He says: "To give kids two moms or two dads is to withhold ... someone whom they desperately need and deserve in order to be whole and happy."

From the book Courageous

One says, "Divorce comes with the territory now." Another responds, "Divorce happens because you make it an option." (page 68)

One says his parents "...were never married ... my dad ... Had six children from three women ... I'm thirty-seven years old, and I have never met my biological father." (pages 68,69)

One explains that men "... have been told abortion is between a woman and her doctor. Well, if I have no say over whether the child even lives, if that's entirely the mother's call, then why should I have anything to do with raising the child? The man is either the father of the child or he isn't – you can't have it both ways." (page 69)

Another man said: "I hooked up with a cheerleader in college. She got pregnant. I told her to take care of it, but she wouldn't do it. I got mad and left her to deal with it herself. She lives just thirty minutes away, but all these years I couldn't bring myself to go see her." (page 172)

This describes typical problems in our society caused by absent and negligent fathers.

The Bible Teaching

God's plan shows children need both a father and a mother.

Proverbs 1:8 – Children should hear the instructions of their fathers and not forsake the law of their mothers. (6:20; 23:22)

Ephesians 6:2,3 – Children should honor their father and the mother

One reason God restricted the sexual union to the marriage of one man and one woman, is so children have a family with **both a father and a mother** to raise them.

(Genesis 1:26-28; 2:24; Luke 2:48,51; Mark 5:40; Leviticus 19:3; Proverbs 30:17; Matthew 15:4; 19:19)

God views fatherlessness as a serious problem.

Deuteronomy 10:18 – God administers justice for the fatherless and the widow...

Psalms 68:5 – A father of the fatherless, a defender of widows, is God in His holy habitation.

Psalms 27:10 – When my father and my mother forsake me, then the Lord will take care of me.

If God is so concerned about children without fathers, what right do we have to deliberately choose to make children fatherless by divorce, cohabitation, single-parenting, or homosexuality?

(Isaiah 1:17; 1:23; 10:2; Psalms 82:3; 10:18; 10:14; 146:9; Deuteronomy 27:19; 14:29; 16:11,14; 24:17; 26:12; 27:19; Jeremiah 7:6; Job 24:3,9; 29:12; 31:21; 5:28; 22:3; James 1:27)

God sets the example of a Father who is present with His people.

Psalm 23:4 – Yea, though I walk through the valley of the shadow of death, I will fear no evil; For You are with me; Your rod and Your staff, they comfort me.

Hebrews 13:5 – He Himself has said, "I will never leave you nor forsake you."

Unlike many fathers, God will never leave or forsake His children. God is not an absent father!

(John 14:23; Deuteronomy 31:6,8; Joshua 1:5,9; Genesis 31:3; Isaiah 43:2)

Fathers should know their children like God seeks to know His children.

John 17:3 – And this is eternal life, that they may know You, the only true God.

John 10:14,27 – I am the good shepherd; and I know My sheep, and am known by My own.

In the movie "The Sound of Music," the father had distanced himself from his children. When he realized his mistake, he said, "I don't **know** my children." How many fathers have made a similar mistake? Do we personally know each one of our children so we love and care for them?

(Philippians 3:8,10; 1 John 5:20; Jeremiah 24:7; Daniel 11:32; Hosea 5:4; 6:6; 1 Corinthians 1:21; 8:3; John 14:23; Galatians 4:9; 1 Timothy 4:5; Titus 1:16; 2 Peter 1:2,3; 1 John 2:14; 3:1; 4:6,7,8)

Fathers should love their children like God loves His children.

1 John 4:7-10 – Beloved, let us love one another, for love is of God; and everyone who loves is born of God and knows God. He who does not love does not know God, for God is love. God made known His love by sending Jesus to die for us.

Luke 15:17-22 – When the prodigal son repented, his father received him with love, affection, and compassion.

God not only knows His children, but He loves and cares for each one. Do we as fathers love and care for each of our children?

(Psalms 103:13; John 14:21-23)

Fathers should seek a harmonious relationship with their children like God seeks fellowship, oneness, and unity with His children.

1 John 1:3 – God desires to have fellowship with His children.

John 17:21 – Jesus prayed that His followers all may be one, "as You, Father, are in Me, and I in You; that they also may be one in Us."

God desires close oneness with each of His children. Do we as fathers seek to develop that relationship with our children?

(1 Corinthians 1:9; Proverbs 17:6)

Fathers should communicate with their children as God does with His children.

Genesis 3:8ff – Before man sinned, God personally walked and talked with man in the garden.

2 Timothy 3:16,17 – Today the Father communicates with us through the Scriptures.

Matthew 6:9 – We communicate to the Father in prayer (Matthew 7:8-11).

Revelation 21:3 – Someday in heaven we will again be in God's personal presence.

When people do not study and pray, they are not communicating with their heavenly Father. They are failing to build a personal relationship. Likewise, when we do not spend time with our children to know and care for them, we are failing to build a personal relationship with them.

In *Courageous* one man concludes: "Any [man] can father a child, but it takes courage to *be* a child's father. To be there for them." (page 172)

Another man read the following quotation: "At the end of his life, no man says, 'I wish I had spent less time with my children.'" (page 332)

The Challenge to Be the Family Provider and Protector

In *Courageous* one man was a good family man but struggled to find employment to provide for them. Being the family provider involves challenges.

The Example of God as Provider

Matthew 7:7-11 – Like an earthly father, our heavenly Father gives good gifts to his children.

James 1:17 – Every good and perfect gift is from our Father.

(Galatians 1:3-4; Matthew 6:8-13,25-34; 10:29; John 15:16; 16:23,24; 1 John 3:9,41; Ephesians 1:3; 5:20)

Earthly Fathers Likewise Should Provide for Their Families.

Luke 11:11 – If a son asks his father for bread, will he give him a stone? Or if he asks for a fish, will he give him a serpent? Fathers should not give children everything they ask for. We should give what is **good** for them: that which contributes to their wellbeing.

1 Timothy 5:8 – If anyone does not provide for his own, and especially for those of his household, he has denied the faith and is worse than an unbeliever.

Earthly fathers demonstrate love by providing what children need. But some fathers refuse to hold down a job. Some use the money they earn to please themselves instead of caring for the family. And some simply desert the family and leave. All such are neglecting their duty as fathers.

And many fathers think they have done their job if they provide material things, but they neglect other important needs. Meeting the needs of children includes spiritual training, guidance, and discipline. Fathers should strive to meet all their children's needs.

(Hebrews 12:4-11; Ephesians 3:14-21; Matthew 7:11; Genesis 37)

The Challenge to Be the Spiritual Leader, Instructor, and Authority Figure

Consider the Problem of Absent or Negligent Fathers

Elizabeth Marquardt, whose parents divorced, studied the effects of divorce.*

One of the things we discovered in our study is that young adults from divorced families were less likely to be religious when they grew up .... They were less likely to be a member of a house of worship. They were less likely to hold a leadership position there. ... The image of God as a father, ... who's there for you, protecting you, supporting and providing for you, is an increasingly unfamiliar experience for a lot of young people today."

* From "The High Cost of Fatherlessness: To Children" by Jeff Johnston

From the book/movie Courageous

One of the men says: "I read that if boys grow up with mothers who attend church and fathers who don't, a huge percentage stop going. But when the father goes to church, even if the mother doesn't, the great majority of boys attend church as adults." (page 298)

One said, "You can't fall asleep at the wheel only to wake up one day and realize that your job or your hobbies have no eternal value, but the souls of your children do." (Page 355)

One read the following quotation from Spurgeon: "Fearless of all consequences, you must do the right ... turn not your back like a coward, but play the man ... Better a brief warfare and eternal rest, than false peace and everlasting torment." (page 332)

The Bible Teaching

The father should exercise authority.

Authority is the right to make rules that others are expected to obey. Modern society rebels against every kind of authority, especially that of fathers. But Scripture teaches that fathers are the head of their family and should use their authority for the good of all. This includes instructing the children.

Matthew 6:9,10 – Our Father in heaven is the ultimate authority figure. His will should be done on earth, as it is in heaven. (7:21; 28:18)

When people think that authority is not a masculine quality or that God should be a ***mother***, they serve a false god. One of the main reasons the Bible describes God as our Father is that God is an authority figure, and authority is primarily a masculine characteristic.

Ephesians 6:4 – And you, fathers, do not provoke your children to wrath, but bring them up in the training and admonition of the Lord.

Fathers should exercise authority and use it wisely for the good of their children. But they should also do so in order to demonstrate to children the true nature of God.

(Colossians 3:13-20)

The father should be a spiritual teacher.

Genesis 18:19 – Abraham commanded his children and his household after him, that they keep the way of the LORD, to do righteousness and justice.

Isaiah 38:19 – The father shall make known [God's] truth to the children.

Ephesians 6:4 – Fathers should bring children up in the training and admonition of the Lord.

Fathers are responsible to train their children to understand God's word. But far too often fathers fail because they are absent or negligent, or because they think this is the responsibility of the mothers. Fathers must take the lead and actively teach their children.

(1 Thessalonians 2:11; Deuteronomy 6:6-9; John 6:44,45; Matthew 6:13; 11:25-27; 16:17; 24:36; John 12:48-50; 15:15,16; Proverbs 1:8; 3:12; 4:1; 23:22)

The father must set a good example.

Learning any task is easier if we can observe others. We learn to drive a car, cook a meal, etc. by example. Children are more likely to be righteous if they can see a good example in their father.

1 Peter 1:14-17 – Be obedient children. Be holy because God is holy. God our Father sets an example of holiness that we should imitate.

1 Kings 15:3 – Abijam walked in the sins of his father. Many such statements can be found regarding kings of Israel and Judah. Children often imitate their parents' sins.

In *Courageous* one man says his dad told him he better never catch him drinking. But his dad had a beer in hand at the time. The son said, "It's kind of hard to respect a hypocrite." (page 68)

God expects fathers to teach the truth to their children, not just by word-of-mouth, but also by proper example. What kind of example does an absent father set? Fathers must be actively involved in their children's lives, showing them how to serve God faithfully.

The father should lead in giving punishments and rewards.

Again, many people in our society rebel against these concepts. Yet, part of the masculine role is to punish children for disobedience and reward them for obedience.

Hebrews 11:6 – Our heavenly Father rewards those who diligently seek Him.

John 15:1-6 – The Father takes away branches that bear no fruit and casts them into the fire.

Hebrews 12:7,9 – If you endure chastening, God deals with you as with sons; for what son is there whom a father does not chasten? Human fathers corrected us, and we paid them respect.

1 Samuel 2:25-30; 3:12-14 – Eli and his family were rejected from being priests because he failed to chastise his sons.

Earthly fathers should properly administer rewards and punishments to our children. When we do so, we help people understand the nature of God.

When police arrested two teen gang members for drug dealing, one officer asked, "Where's your daddy?" The teen answered, "Ain' got no daddy."

Another teen, when asked why he got involved with the gang, answered, "I ain't got nobody, man. I just ain't got nobody." (page 344)

Negligent and absent fathers leave their children vulnerable to the evils of society: gangs, drugs, sexual immorality, and false teaching in schools and in religion. Fathers are responsible to guide and protect their children by instruction and discipline.

(Proverbs 13:24; Luke 15:11ff; Matthew 18:35; 1 Peter 1:7)

Conclusion

In *Courageous* one man bought a new suit. When he put it on, he said, "I feel like a rich man." His wife responded, "... you *are* a rich man. You have a strong faith, two children that love you, and a wife that adores you" (pages 184,185). No amount of money, financial investments, or long hours on the job can purchase these riches. They come only from dedication to developing good family relations and good spiritual leadership based on God's word.

The book ends as one man challenges men to accept the responsibility of fatherhood. He says:

> You don't have to ask who will guide my family because by God's grace, *I* will. You don't have to ask who will teach my son to follow Christ because *I* will. Who will accept the responsibility of providing for and protecting my family? ... *I am their father; I will.* ... I want the favor of God and His blessing on my home. ... fathers who fear the Lord ... It's time to rise up and answer the call that God has given to you and say, I will! I will! *I will!"* (page 356)

Joshua 24:15 – We must say with Joshua, "As for me and my house, we will serve the LORD."

Sources:

https://www.focusonthefamily.com/socialissues/marriage/high-cost-of-fatherlessness/high-cost-of-fatherlessness-to-all-of-us

https://www.focusonthefamily.com/socialissues/marriage/high-cost-of-fatherlessness/high-cost-to-fatherlessness-to-children

"The Father Absence Crisis in America," National Fatherhood Initiative

Printed books, booklets, and tracts available at
www.gospelway.com/sales
Free Bible study articles online at
www.gospelway.com
Free Bible courses online at
www.biblestudylessons.com
Free class books at
www.biblestudylessons.com/classbooks
Free commentaries on Bible books at
www.biblestudylessons.com/commentary
Contact the author at
www.gospelway.com/comments
Free e-mail Bible study newsletter –
www.gospelway.com/update_subscribe.htm

Made in the USA
Middletown, DE
28 October 2022